THE SUZUKI CONCEPT:

AN INTRODUCTION TO A SUCCESSFUL METHOD
FOR EARLY MUSIC EDUCATION

By
Shinichi Suzuki, Elizabeth Mills, Mae Ferro, Marian Schreiber
Louise Behrend, Anastasia Jempelis, John Kendall,
Harlow Mills, Margaret Rowell, Diana Tillson,
and the American Suzuki Institute—West

Edited by
Elizabeth Mills and Sr. Therese Cecile Murphy
with an Introduction by Dr. Masaaki Honda

"We are the children of our environment."

S. Suzuki

diablo press

© 1973 DIABLO PRESS, Inc.
Berkeley and San Francisco
462 Coventry Road, Berkeley, California 94707

September 1973

Library of Congress Catalog Card Number: 72-97891

ISBN 0-87297-002-7 Cloth Edition
ISBN 0-87297-003-5 Paper Edition

The publisher is grateful to Dr. Shinichi Suzuki and to the Summy-Birchard Company for their permission to reproduce copyright materials.

Printed in the United States of America

Preface

This book originated with the American Suzuki Institute—West, which presented its first seminars in 1972 at Holy Names College, Oakland. The Institute was designed to stimulate teachers and families already at work with the Suzuki concept, but its astonishing popularity caused it to include introductory materials as well.

This sudden rise to popularity was not new for the Suzuki concept in the United States. In 1958 a Japanese student at Oberlin College brought to America a film showing an ensemble of a thousand Japanese children playing Bach's Double Concerto. They were among the tens of thousands of children who had been taught to play the violin by Shinichi Suzuki and his followers. The film so amazed people that a "Suzuki explosion" took place in the United States. Music educators led by Clifford Cook of Oberlin Conservatory, John Kendall of Southern Illinois University, Howard Van Sickle of Mankato College, Minnesota, and Alfred Garson in Canada founded the Suzuki movement in North America.

In 1959 Mr. Kendall became the first American teacher to study with Dr. Suzuki* in Japan. Many others followed. In 1964, Dr. Suzuki brought a group of children to perform at the Music Educators' National Conference in Philadelphia. The delegates saw first-hand the remarkable results of his teaching. Until 1970 he came to the United States each summer to present workshops in universities and conservatories.

After spreading quickly, the Suzuki concept took root in the United States. In 1966 the Eastman School of Music,

---

*Dr. Suzuki holds honorary degrees from three universities in North America.

with funding from the National Endowment for the Arts and the New York State Council on the Arts, established a testing and instrumental program to adapt Suzuki principles to string teaching in American public schools. In 1967 a non-profit organization, Talent Education USA, Inc., was founded. In 1972 it was expanded and became the Suzuki Association of the Americas. And each October since 1966 Dr. Masaaki Honda and Kenji Mochizuki, the student who brought the first film to Oberlin, accompany ten Suzuki students from Japan on an annual Talent Education Tour of North America.

Thousands of American children now are studying by the Suzuki method. In Japan the method is used to teach not only the violin, but the piano, cello, flute, koto, art, and related subjects, and there are well-established centers for its use in more than 50 cities. As the number of Suzuki students multiplies in the United States it has become certain that the method will have a profound effect not only on American string instruction, but on basic educational philosophy as well. This book offers a concise description of the method, explaining through essays and dialogues of leading teachers its philosophy, psychology, history, and applications to the violin, piano, and cello.

Successful performances often before audiences, help young students to gain confidence.

Contents

About the Contributors

Dr. Shinichi Suzuki is a master violin teacher, an educational philosopher of penetrating perceptions, and a great humanitarian. Eight years of study in the Berlin of the 1920's prepared him for the professional life which was to follow in Japan. His astounding success with very young children led to the growth of the movement which has become known throughout the world as Talent Education, which has gathered momentum first in post-war Japan, then during the sixties in the Americas, and now in the seventies is spreading to Europe. Countless students and their parents have had their lives enriched by this approach, which combines the qualities of virtually universal applicability and highest artistic standards. The headquarters of his work (where children of that area receive regular training under teachers he has trained and where he trains further teachers from Japan and other countries) is the Talent Education Institute in Matsumoto, Japan.

Elizabeth Mills is director of the Pasadena Talent Education Program which serves more than 250 students of violin, cello, and piano under a staff of affiliated private Suzuki teachers. As a well-known concert violinist and teacher, she became one of the early exponents of Suzuki's philosophy, making several trips to Japan and attending his various workshops in the U.S. She has also taken part in extending the work by conducting teacher workshops in several colleges.

Mae Ferro is teacher therapist at the Raskob Learning Institute, Oakland, where her special project is to teach reading to educationally handicapped children. She is also an instructor in the special education department at Holy Names College, Oakland.

Marian Schreiber is a member of the faculty at the Community Music School of Greater Vancouver. She is Director there of the Suzuki Program, which includes more than 200 students. A pioneer in the introduction of the Suzuki Method to the United States, she has conducted seven Suzuki workshops. She is also a widely known violinist who studied under Boris Sirpo, Mischel Piastro, and Emanuel Zetlin, as well as with Dr. Suzuki.

Louise Behrend is a member of the faculty, Julliard School of Music, New York. A violinist who studied in Washington and at the Mozarteum, Salzburg, Austria, she made her Town Hall debut in 1950 and has since given many performances and demonstrations throughout the world. She is founder and director of the School for Strings, a Suzuki program for students and teachers.

Anastasia Jempelis is director of the Suzuki Program at the Eastman School of Music in Rochester, New York. There Dr. Suzuki guided the training of American teachers over the two-year period of Project Super, which was jointly funded by the New York State Council of the Arts and the National Endowment of the Arts. She is a noted violinist and educator who has often given performances and demonstrations of the Suzuki methods.

John Kendall is Professor of String Development at Southern Illinois University. A pioneer in the introduction of the Suzuki Method to the United States, he has traveled to 40 states to give lectures, demonstrations, and workshops on string teaching. His books and records, "Listen and Play," are based on Dr. Suzuki's ideas and are widely used by American teachers.

Harlow Mills is well-known in the musical life of Southern California as a pianist, teacher, and the long-time manager of the Coleman Chamber Music Association. He graduated from the Curtis Institute of Music in Philadelphia. Having observed the results of the Suzuki work by his wife, Elizabeth Mills, he became interested in incorporating it into his own teaching, and went to Japan to observe the work when the piano method books were published.

Margaret Rowell is head of the cello departments of three institutions: Stanford University, the University of California, and the San Francisco Conservatory of Music. As concert cellist she was a member of the Arion Trio and for ten years with the Concert Trio on NBC radio. She is co-author of the cello book of Paul Rolland's "Prelude to String Playing."

Diana Tillson is Music Coordinator of the Bedford School District, New York. She has studied the violin, trumpet, and French horn and has received orchestral training at Salzburg, the University of Vienna, the University of Paris, the Boston Symphony, the Philadelphia Orchestra, the National Orchestral Association, and the Berkshire Music School. Dr. Suzuki is among her many distinguished teachers.

Phyllis W. Glass is Professor of Music, University of Southern California, Los Angeles, California, where she established the Suzuki-Early Development Program. She served as president of the American String Teachers Association, California unit, for four years, and as national secretary of ASTA for four years. In 1971 she studied violin with Dr. Suzuki in Matsumoto and in the same year studied with master cellists in Japan.

Margery Aber is Assistant Professor of Music and Music Education at the State University of Wisconsin, a member of the music faculty at Gesell Institute, a Director of the American Suzuki Institute, a private music teacher, and a Talent Education teacher in the Extension Division, Department of Music, University of Wisconsin, Madison. For 25 years she taught music in the public schools of Detroit, Michigan.

Yvonne M. Tait is on the staff of the Tucson Public Schools and has been Professor of Cello and Music Theory at Baylor University, Oklahoma State University, Illinois Wesleyan University, and the National Music Camp. She has participated in Suzuki workshops at Southern Illinois University, Eastman School of Music, and in Tucson.

Dr. Masaaki Honda is a pediatrician and pioneer of the Talent Education movement, as well as a leader in organizing the more recent expansion of the work into the Early Development Association which is more comprehensive in scope than music alone. He received his early education in San Francisco before returning to Japan to live. Serving as spokesman, he has accompanied the annual tours of young Suzuki musicians to America and Europe.

ADDITIONAL CONTRIBUTORS ARE AS FOLLOWS:

American Suzuki Institute—West Faculty: William Starr, Suzuki Pedagogy Specialist, University of Tennessee; Mihoko Yamaguchi, Suzuki-trained Specialist, Matsumoto, Japan; Suzuki Center, Seattle, Wash.; Constance Starr, Instructor in Piano, University of Tennessee; Theodore Brunson, Alison Corson, Sister Bridget of Mary Furlong, Atsuko Konishi, Shirlene McMichael and Sister Catherine Rauch.

Photographs of the Wisconsin Suzuki Institute which appear in this book are by Arthur Montzka. Other photographs are by John Blaustein and John Wright.

Introduction

Dr. Masaaki Honda

*"We must express (our movement) as a total
human education."*

Shinichi Suzuki visited Germany at the age of 18 to study
violin under Prof. Karl Klingler.The difficulty he encountered
was not in violin but in language. He was surprised to notice
that all German children at the age of three understood and
spoke fluent German. Though people took this phenomenon
for granted as a natural thing, it struck him that children's
potentialities must be demonstrated in absorbing things from
their environment. If they can speak and understand such
difficult things as language, they surely must have the abilities
for performing high arts if these are also developed at a tender
age. Thus he applied this idea in teaching violin.

The first presentation of Dr. Suzuki's pupils was held in
1942 in Tokyo. At that time, of course, the system was not
called the Suzuki Method or the organization named Talent
Education. A few years before this time Dr. Suzuki began
teaching violin to young children. He noticed that all children,
contrary to the general concept, developed their abilities in
playing violin regardless of hereditary ingenuity.

After World War II, Dr. Suzuki began teaching children in
Matsumoto, Japan, and in the year 1947, the Talent Education
Institute was organized. Up to this time, and even today, the
general concept of the word "talent" was that of a particular
faculty with which one is naturally endowed. Talent Educa-

tion is based on the assumption that humans are born with a very high potential for developing themselves. Dr. Suzuki's observation of the wonderful results among children as they learned their mother tongues was the basis. Children in all parts of the world have developed this wonderful language ability which is developed by environment. What they receive from their parents at the day of birth is not music or language, but the ability to learn and speak language or perform music. If the babies have no physical defects, all are born with these qualities. Thus, our concept of this word talent is the same ability, which means there is the possibility of raising various abilities in all human beings to a very high standard.

But our understanding of this phrase "Talent Education" applies not only to knowledge or technical skill but also to morality, building of character, and appreciating beauty. We know that these are human attributes acquired by education and environment. Thus our movement is not concerned with raising so-called prodigies, nor does it intend to emphasize just "early development." We must express it as a "total human education."

How It Affects Children

I think it is clear now that the aim in Talent Education is not to make musicians. We should not set a road for the future of children. They should make their own choice of profession at a suitable age, and may choose music or another field. Our main purpose is merely to establish a foundation for the future character. Music is one of the best methods to develop various qualities in a human being.

The violin as an instrument for study has certain advantages:
1. There are various sizes from 1/16 to full size, matching the physical stature of each child.
2. Correct tones require precise fingering.
3. Absolute pitch may be developed.
4. Bowing requires a sensitive grip and develops tonal sense.

2

As a regular part of Suzuki training, students play among friends who share their interests and skills. This encourages musical development.

5. Memory abilities are developed through the playing of all music from memory (which is important also in freeing the child's attention so that he may concentrate on posture, technique, and pitch).
6. Concentration and perseverance are required and developed.
7. A high degree of sensitivity is developed.
8. Appreciation of the fine musical literature for violin will extend naturally to symphonic and other literature.

These qualities are important in any profession they will follow in the future.

Mother's Help

Mothers should always attend the lessons with their children. As children receive only one lesson a week, the mother must instruct the children during the other six days. The mother's role is very important in developing the abilities. They would be much more difficult to achieve without her. As they have

3

a common project, there is little chance of a generation or communication gap between them when they grow older.

It might be the mother who is the most important person in this movement. Of course, most of the mothers have never played a violin before starting their child on this instrument. Their knowledge of the instrument and sensitivity to music develops on a parallel with the children.

Manners

Good manners are requested at lessons. In Japan children bow to the teacher before the lesson and say "thank you" afterwards. There is a story of a three year old girl who had eye trouble and visited a clinic. It was near noon and the doctor and nurse were tired and frustrated after consulting more than forty patients. The doctor looked at the next paper and said "next." The girl went up by the desk and, bowing to the doctor, said "Good morning. Will you please help me?" The doctor looked up, and seeing the little girl, with all his weariness, could not but smile. The atmosphere in the room changed. After her treatment, the girl having withstood the pain, again bowed and said "thank you." The doctor smiled again and said "Thanks to you. Please come again."

Worldwide Spread of the Suzuki Concept

Since we first brought children from Japan to demonstrate in the U.S.A. in 1964, the idea has spread in various parts of the country, and thousands of children are receiving lessons. The people in this country not only appreciate the method but understand the philosophy, and I cannot but respect the American people.

In 1966 we visited Canada for the first time and many classes have developed there too. In 1970 the first tour to England was undertaken, and we had a concert and workshop at the Royal College of Music in London. Teachers from all parts of England, as well as from Ireland and Holland attended here. B.B.C. made video pictures which were shown throughout the country, helping spread the idea. In 1971, concerts and workshops were held in Queen Elizabeth Hall in London, and in halls in Birmingham, Cheshire, Sheffield, and in Scotland. Receiving reports from Mrs. Stephen Moore, general secretary of the School Music Association, I understood it was a huge success.

Now we have just finished our third visit to England on route to the U.S., and I observed that this movement is firmly taking root. In 1970 when I talked on the stage, they seemed suspicious and a little skeptical. After this year's visit, I felt the change in the atmosphere. They were understanding and enthusiastic. I felt the warm feeling of the audience and the reception was very good. But it was still expressed that perhaps the movement was successful in Japan because it was carried out by Japanese mothers. The British mothers, they said, were too busy and probably cannot do the same with their children. These remarks were heard also in the U.S. ten years ago. Visits have been made to Germany and Sweden and Portugal, but though they showed a great deal of interest, results have yet not come from these countries.

Early Development Association

In 1969 a new non-profit body called Early Development Association was established in Japan. Mr. Masaru Ibuka, the founder of the well known Sony Corporation, became the chairman of the new organization. He has influenced some of the most prominent business men in Japan to join the Board.

The aim of this organization is to apply the ideas of Talent Education to other fields beside music. Research investigation is being carried out with children in the following classes: drawing, calligraphy, Japanese and English, gymnastics and "thinking" (basics of mathematics). Drawing is fundamentally different from learning music. Creation and vision are demanded in this field and so children are allowed to draw pictures freely at the first stage. But when a child comes to a certain period, he must be taught to recognize and reproduce more accurately a tree's shape and color. Up to this point, though many might draw a tree's shape as a triangle and the color black, it was all right. Next they are taught to draw it as it is. Our aim is not to make professional painters, but it is important to learn to copy a specimen correctly. This ability is important in various professions they may follow in the future.

Japanese characters are very difficult to learn and it will probably seem like magic to a foreigner observing native people writing in the Kanji (originally Chinese characters) very easily. These consist of more complex patterns than ordinary alphabets with which several words must be combined to make any meaning. Children are taught a very few words at the beginning, and adding one word to another, they will learn hundreds of words within two or three years easily.

English is very difficult to Japanese as well as Japanese to Americans. Groups consisting of 15 children are taught entirely by ear by an American teacher speaking only English. They begin from very simple words like, "Hello, hello. This is Kathy," and proceed to a more difficult sentence. Ten tapes are available containing all the lessons. In tapes 3, 6 and 9 there are poems which will be the checking points. Children are requested to memorize all these words and sentences by listening to the tapes at their homes. The instructor teaches 45 minutes once a week. The instructor teaches the sentences with action and with pictures to illustrate.

The Thinking class is a combination of various lessons. Children learn numbers, and by using sticks or marbles, will be lead to think what combinations, for example, will add up to nine: 5 plus 4 = 9, 6 plus 3 = 9, etc. They are also taught how to read a sentence which generally consists of descriptions like "sky is blue," "Trees are green," "water is clear," etc. This connects to their daily lives and leads to the sensitivity also, to appreciate the beauty of nature.

The ages of the children coming to these classes range from

2-6. It is a little difficult for a two year old child to concentrate for 45 minutes, so generally they are accepted at age 3, but there was an interesting case of a girl named "Mami" who attended English class at the age of 9 months. She was always in her mother's arms, neither speaking nor showing any sign of understanding. After 7 months, when the instructor took the children individually to check each child's progress, this little girl was among the best in speaking and hearing. She had been accumulating what she had observed over the 7 months.

The Early Development Association is not trying to develop an elite group of children. Our education is not only for well-to-do families who can afford to come and also have the motivation. The ultimate aim is to send the curriculum and materials to homes, where they are really needed. The natural place for early education is in the home. Our studies are still in a very early stage. We hope to study in more different fields, and with many classes of children.

People were very slow to realize that children have such great potential for musical expression. They didn't expect a little child to produce a serious and beautiful style, phrasing, and interpretation in music. That is the one thing that astonishes everyone who hears children trained by Dr. Suzuki. People weep, drop their jaws, mutter, "I don't believe it; it's not possible; it's a trick."

Louise Behrend

This girl, who first held a violin before the age of three, now is a talented violinist. The Suzuki concept has been a powerful force in her growth.

Chapter 1

Children Can Develop Their Ability to the Highest Standard

Shinichi Suzuki

". . . I have developed a method for the education of 'genius.'"

If all parents were awakened to the inherent nature of their children and provided them with an ideal environment, all children would gain extraordinary ability. Among the children of the world, there are no exceptions. I began to build my life around this theory more than thirty years ago, and today it is being proved true. With the increasing success of this concept I feel an irresistible urge to tell everyone that children's growth depends on how they are raised. Education begins from the day of birth.

The Incomparable Quality of Children at Birth

We are often asked to believe that human ability is given by nature, but in fact it is developed. The cultural level of children in the Stone Age was very low, yet this does not mean that people in those days were all dull by nature. If they had been dull, our ancestors in the Stone Age would have been morons. The fact is that they were not morons, but were influenced by the environment of that time. They grew to be men of their times.

I believe that vitality, the driving force of all human ability, determines the quality of man at birth. Therefore, it is wrong to conclude that people have or lack ability because of what they have or gained later. No one can tell how able man is by nature. What is known is the ability that is spoiled or developed.

Careless Parents

We must never forget that certain talents can be developed when a certain environment is provided. Too many parents are misled by the words "born musician" or "born painter." They believe that talent is latent in children. They think their children have no talent if they see no ability in them as infants.

What living creatures will become depends on the very first stage of their development. Man is no exception. One's future fate, or his ability in later life, is determined by his training in infancy and childhood. Everyone knows that a young plant cannot achieve growth without proper attention. Careless parents do not realize that their children will lose their ability as they grow unless they are exposed to a proper environment, just like young plants.

Parents often let the precious days go by. They try to educate their children when it is too late. Finally they give up with the excuse, "Well, it seems that my boy was born without talent." These parents fully deserve to be called careless, for they have let the youngster's only chance slip by. Yet they talk of talent as though it could not be developed by careful upbringing.

I am inclined to think that, in this present age, not all children are being trained properly. In fact, very few of them are raised as they should be. Their inborn nature often is neglected.

Children's Ability is Surprising

In considering the inborn nature of human beings we ought to give deep thought to the nature of a baby on the day of its birth. I did so one day about thirty years ago and made a discovery that overwhelmed me. I discovered that all children, throughout the world, are educated to speak their native languages with the utmost fluency. This education in their native languages enables them to develop their linguistic abilities successfully to an extremely high level.

It cannot be denied that most children speak their language beautifully. A six-year-old Japanese child knows about 3,000 to 4,000 words; English and American children, and those of all other nations, quickly become proficient in speech. Is this not an astonishing fact? All children show their splendid capacity by speaking and understanding their mother tongue. There is no clearer demonstration of the original power of the human mind.

Children everywhere are educated by a method which has been in continuous practice throughout all human history. A child's abilities develop by being developed. This fact proves that the talent of every child can be developed. The world's best educational method, in other words, is found in the method of teaching the mother tongue. This is what I have been studying, and I have developed a method for the education of "genius."

Even the youngest children find in music a means of expressing deep emotions.

SUZUKI CONCEPT

Method of Talent Education

Through this method I have trained four- and five-year old children to play many Vivaldi violin concertos. I think this is only natural, for children have such a talent by nature. It needs only to be developed. Cultural sensitivity is not inherited. It is learned. Any child will display highly superior abilities if only the correct methods are used in training and developing these abilities.

The method of education which I have been using is nothing but the method of education in the native language, applied without any essential modifications in musical education. There are two principles which I regard as the most important elements in this method:

1) The child must be helped to develop an ear for music.
2) From the very beginning, every step must by all means be thoroughly mastered.

In the past it was generally believed that an ear for music is innate. The ability of all children to learn both speech and music, however, shows that it is a talent that can be learned. An ear for music is something which can be acquired by listening, and the sooner this is begun the more effective it will be. An ear for music is not innate. It is a human aptitude which can only be developed by listening.

I invite you to try it. Select one piece of great music for a newborn baby. Train the baby by letting him listen every day to a record or a tape recording of the same piece of music. The baby is made to listen to only one piece repeatedly. If this is done it will be found that any baby, after five or six months, will show recognition of this piece of music. If the child is brought up day after day in this atmosphere of good music, there can be no doubt that he will eventually become a young person with an excellent ear for music. This experiment has already been carried out successfully by hundreds of families.

By the same token, if a baby is brought up listening day after day to a melody played off-key by a tone-deaf person, then any baby brought up under such families would not develop a good musical ear. Repetition will produce a poor, as well as a good ear.

Music educators can no longer regard an ear for music as incapable of development. There is no such thing as an innate aptitude for music. In place of this concept I have proposed the following: "Abilities are born and develop by the workings of the vital forces of the organism as it strives to live and to adjust to its environment." Of course there are individuals who are born with inherently superior or inferior qualities, and differences in ability will no doubt occur because of these innate differences. But it is my belief that innate superiority or inferiority is basically nothing but a relatively superior or inferior ability to adjust to environmental conditions.

Education for the development of an ear for music should form a part of all musical education, whether private teaching or musical instruction. I recommend the following method: the piece to be learned should always be played beforehand to the pupils every day by means of records or tape recordings. This will develop the ear. The pupils should continue to listen to the records or tapes while they are learning the piece. Of course, the recordings should be superior performances of the music.

It may safely be predicted that the ear for music will develop in direct proportion to the number of times that the piece is heard. This method may even be effective if the music is played in the room while the pupils are studying another subject, for instance, arithmetic. As long as the music is audible the life forces of the human being will unconsciously absorb it, making it part of the individual abilities.

I feel strongly that this concept is the most important element in musical education. I am sure that some day it will be accepted all over the world. It cannot be otherwise, for the results have been revealed. However, one must not expect far-reaching results after only short periods. Musical sense develops gradually and imperceptibly, just as linguistic sense does. The same is true of the learning of speech patterns. Children who grow up in Boston will by an imperceptible process become speakers with a Boston lilt, while those of New York will learn another one.

A Rule for Developing True Early Talent

While the first principle, listening, guides the pupil, the second guides the teacher when the pupil is very young. It is: "From the very beginning every step must by all means be thoroughly mastered." This is one of the most important elements in developing performing techniques.

There are some teachers who go immediately from one piece to the next as soon as the pupil has learned to play. Many of these teachers become failures. This system concentrates on increasing the number of pieces learned, rather than on what is really important—the development of ability.

Beginning musicians are particularly vulnerable to the pressure to accumulate pieces. They should be encouraged to master each piece. There is a certain period when the pupil has finally become able to play his first piece. I call this the time when the pupil is "prepared." I say: "Now the lessons really begin. From now on your abilities will really develop." From this point I train the pupil intensively and continue until he has attained thorough mastery.

Let us suppose that the pupil has become able to play *Piece A* well. At this time I will add *Piece B*. We will then work on Piece B while still continuing to work on Piece A. The lesson will include both pieces. As soon as *Piece C* has been added the emphasis on Piece A will be reduced: the lessons will consist of Pieces A, B, and C. This is the method by which I teach beginners. In this way the skills accumulated will become an ever-increasing reservoir of greater ability, making possible further great advances.

Five Conditions for Genius Education

If parents want to bring up their children to have outstanding

Learning music well helps children to establish a healthy self-image that continues to serve them when they begin to study other disciplines.

ability they should pay attention to the following points:

1) Educate as early as possible.
2) Give as much training as possible.
3) Create as favorable an environment as possible.
4) Have as good teachers as possible.
5) Adopt as good an educational method as possible.

Wise affection creates wise children, while foolish affection makes foolish children. The talent of every child can be developed. Every one of us should spread this way of thinking with a sincere desire to help wise parents, especially those who want to raise children of pure minds and excellent chances.

My Message to the United States

I sincerely urge you to conduct a mighty educational movement to develop an ear for music in all American children.

15

Today, when we have records and tapes, this method of education may be carried out anywhere. The most important thing of all is to conduct a social movement to encourage parents to give their children an ear for music from the time when the children are still babies. If only this practice in the home were to become a matter accepted as common sense it would undoubtedly solve our music problems in the school. Wonderful results could be attained.

How is it possible for us to give music education to children who have been made tone-deaf in their homes? Musical aptitude is not inborn.

Not only in music, but in many other fields children are often educated in ways which stunt and damage their abilities. I believe that attention must be given to a child's education from the day of his birth. Educators are often presented with pupils whose correct education has been neglected, whose abilities have been impaired, and who have been turned into pitifully stunted, thwarted children. When confronted with such pupils, educators in the past were often inclined to think that such children were born with innately inferior abilities.

Today the time has come when we must reject this attitude as an erroneous one. Every child, except a baby one day old, is what he is because of what he has been taught. The abilities displayed by any child are the results of the training which he has been given in the past.

Let us work together to build a new human race. I urge you to explore and develop new paths for the education of children so that all American children, through your efforts, will be given the happiness which they deserve.

Pablo Casals said: "It may very well be music which will save the world." These words express perfectly the hopes for the future of mankind by all persons engaged in music. And I am profoundly convinced that this is the mission that has been laid upon our shoulders.

Chapter 2

Advice To A New Mother

Elizabeth Mills

"Dr. Suzuki . . . does say unreservedly that (through his concept) any child can learn to play beautifully, and in so doing will gain greater dignity and happiness."

Dear Sheila,

Congratulations on the birth of your son. You've asked me to help you to teach him the joys of music. If music education begins on the first day of life, as Dr. Suzuki says, you, as his mother, have an extraordinary responsibility. In our society, your helpless infant is in your complete charge. It is for you either to nurture or to dissipate his enormous musical potential.

Dr. Suzuki says that "abilities are born and developed by the working of the vital forces of an organism as it strives to live and to adjust to its environment." In this view the ideal of music education, therefore, is to assist every child to make his own adjustment in as rich and creative a way as possible. To Dr. Suzuki the terms "superior" and "inferior" talent indicate only the relative success of the adjustment. This means that you have an awesome opportunity—to do nothing at all is the only complete failure.

How can you help your child to develop the talent that is his birthright? The success of the Suzuki method in Japan is closely related to the willingness of parents to give their children music in the earliest stages of life. Just as the infant is exposed to the spoken language he is exposed to music. In

The mother plays an important role in daily teaching. The result is often a closer bond between mother and child. This was a scene at the Wisconsin Institute.

one superb description, he should be given a "musical bath" every day. If the music is of high quality and the same piece is used, he will begin to develop an "ear" for music at once. He will soon begin to respond to what he has repeatedly heard. I suggest a movement of perhaps a Vivaldi or Mozart work as being appropriate for you and your son.

Just as he will learn language because you speak to him, he can learn music, if you set an example. Throughout his early years, establish a musical relationship with him. Attend lessons with him when he is about three. Learn how to hold the violin and the bow properly, and how to play the first simple melody. Naturally, he will want to imitate you. Step-by-step he will learn how to hold a tiny violin and to produce the notes of the now-familiar tune with the bow. The steps are small. What I once thought was a single step I now realize was twenty.

Other mothers and their children will usually be present during the lesson. This will encourage freedom in playing before others, and the audience will be given the benefit of extra learning through observation. Suzuki students are urged from the outset to help each other rather than to compete.

One of the most exciting things about becoming involved in a good Suzuki type program is the opportunity to become part of a real community of parents and children who provide a stimulating and encouraging environment in which your child will thrive. Not only your child will develop—you and Bob will find help in growing as parents from the others who have been in the program long enough to help you over the hurdles. If at times you feel guilty when other children forge ahead faster than your own, console yourself that at least it is better for you to feel guilty than for Bobby! Corrosive guilt is too defeatist, but analyze what you've done and compare with the procedures of some of the more "successful mothers" you know. It may be that Bobby isn't well, that he has reached a temporary plateau, or just that he has reached a point in the repertoire where nearly every student slows down and parents become discouraged. Find out what the teacher thinks. He may recommend more record listening, or additional group work to motivate him, or some tutoring sessions with an older student to whom he is attracted.

Let me hear from you occasionally about Bobby's growth—both physical and musical. Perhaps you, too, will notice more about music as you listen to "his records" repeatedly. Here's to a life made richer by music.

Yours sincerely,

Elizabeth

Dear Sheila,

It's hard to believe that the time has come for Bobby to begin his violin lessons. According to what you have written me from time to time, I gather that he *has* become strongly musical. Isn't it a thrill when a very young child can sing the Bach Minuets from hearing them on the first Suzuki record? Those Bach pieces really appeal to the toddlers. Of course, if he couldn't sing them it would only prove that he couldn't sing—not that he couldn't hear. But a child who can sing well has

19

certainly proven that he *hears* well. Keep up that singing, as well as hearing the music he is to learn, and riding in the car is an excellent time to utilize.

As you face, as an adult, the necessity for practice, remember that he can face it only as a child. That means that it will be as informal as playing with toys, and that his attention span will vary as much as his interest in most toys does. Seize the moment, and know that he may learn a tremendous concept in a few seconds. You may coax his attention back after it wanders, but the quality of work will not be the same. Be happy with two minutes, and wait for other moments during the day, working gradually to develop a pattern of using what become the best periods for him (not for *your* schedule, necessarily).

During practice sessions or in discussions of music, help your child to understand the importance of music in his life. Avoid forcing or bribing. Dr. Suzuki suggests that it's better to give your child a treat at the beginning of practice rather than at the end. A gesture of this kind precludes any hint that you will withhold affection if your son does not play well. Of course, you will love him whether or not he is a fine violinist, and you must show him that.

Instead of criticizing your son, support him. Find things to enjoy and to approve of in his playing. No matter how many mistakes he makes, there will always be something to praise. Children have surprisingly high standards when they begin their lessons—even pre-schoolers; and they are easily frustrated by the unexpected revelation of flaws in their playing. One child was unwilling or unable to accept responsibility for the sounds that came from his violin. He pushed it away, crying, "I'm never going to play *that* violin again. It has a squeak in it!" His friends couldn't persuade him that the violin was blameless. He wasn't ready to learn, except on his own terms. Another child put it succinctly: "I want to *know* how to play. I don't want to *learn* how."

Playing the repertory, at least through the "Perpetual

Motion," is one of the best ways to be helpful. Even those who've never played an instrument before, find it entertaining and in some ways easy. This will guarantee not only that you will appreciate your child's efforts, but that you will enjoy professional concerts more yourself. You will understand the importance of the bowing as the main factor in tone production and musical heart. You will understand the part that a well-shaped and responsive left hand plays in keeping the notes in tune. You will learn how helpless a good ear is unless the fingers also "hear." In fact, you'll be sure to wonder whether you can develop sensitivity for the position of your fingers on the strings. Most of all, you will enjoy yourself, your experience with the music, and your new relationship with your child.

Children of school age often think the attempts of their parents to play are hilarious. Their own egos are increased by the fact that they are able to learn so much more rapidly than the parents can. When they get to the point where they begin to slow down because of lack of experience or strength, or because they can't handle so many details at once, they may notice that their parents are improving greatly. This impresses them and helps them to live with their own mistakes. It gives them hope and a glimpse of what the learning process is like. That's a great family experience.

If you were a string player, you would have a different set of problems, for in all probability, your child would resent your help more than if you knew nothing at all. You would have to fight to avoid quick gasps when he is clumsy or makes a mistake. All parents, musicians or not, will need to learn to hold their tongues when shocked to see a violin fall to the floor. Young children are accustomed to dropping toys, too. It's just one of life's tasks to learn to hang on to something properly, and an outraged cry from a parent just makes the child uncomfortable in a bewildered way. A little educating is in order, but one must remember that the instrument is more expendable than your child's continued happiness in the musical experience. The bridge may fall, a peg may be jolted loose, but small sized violins seldom break.

In the fullness of your wisdom you may be tempted to say, "That's the wrong side of the bridge," at some point. Avoid it. Let him discover on which side of the bridge his tone is more buttery. He probably is well aware of it anyway and is just having fun being "wrong," He isn't stupid. After all, his way of determining right and wrong is far more scientific and probably more productive than if he merely followed rules as a substitute for experience. And you can also remind yourself that at least he will know all about producing some of the strange sounds called for in current *avant garde* music.

In general, go easy on the verbal advice. Put the child in a situation where he is more likely to pull the bow the right way or to hold the violin at the correct angle. If it seems necessary to stop him in the middle of something, don't shout "No!" End his playing for the moment with a gentle, "O.K., fine, How about doing it this way?"

You may be able to play with him in a variety of ways that will make his playing experience more exciting. Before playing

In many regions the parents of all students attend a weekly workshop. This one is led by Kiyo Tashima, a mother who studied the violin and became a teacher.

composed duets with him harmonize together while he plays the variations on open strings. Just playing the rhythms, too, but on a different chord tone, will sound very satisfying. Expand the possibilities as you gain experience, and then go on to the duet parts that are available in a separate Suzuki book. Since you play the piano, think through the differences between your instrument and your son's. Don't assume that practice methods helpful on the piano are equally so on the violin. Playing slowly on the piano, for example, makes many things easier. On the violin it complicates the bowing, as it would a singer's breath control. Slow practice is not a panacea for violinists, valuable as it often is.

The most important single factor in practice has to do with quickly timed preparation of both hands for each note. Generally, the left-hand finger must be in place a split second before the bow moves. This takes much practice. An invaluable practice method consists of quick bow pauses as a finger is placed for the next tone. Remember that on the violin the player has control of the beginning, middle, and end of each tone. Another difference between the violin and the piano is that the violinist has fine control of pitch, measured by the smallest moves of the finger. As little as 1/32-inch move will change the pitch. Fingers must have memories for spacing, too, since each interval (or distance between notes) along the length of the string is smaller than the preceding one. Be thrilled when a phrase is in tune. Be patient when it is not. And encourage every bit of progress, resisting the temptation to become discouraged.

You will also discover the problems of having to hold and play an instrument at the same time. It may be relaxing to sit down at a piano and run your fingers over the keys, but after going through the violin preliminaries—opening up, rosining the bow, tuning the strings, putting on a shoulder pad—you may begin your labors by taking a firm grip on the violin between the jawbone and collarbone. As if that weren't enough, you then twist your left arm around so that the hand faces backward. The other arm then must start moving the bow with an entirely different set of sensations. You will remember, as you learn to play the violin, that you spent the first part of your life trying to get your hands together on some object, and now you are trying to get them to work separately. Naturally, this is an illusion: they still must work together, constantly, to produce each single sound.

If this sounds complicated and awkward, relax. It quickly becomes second nature if you come to terms with these problems immediately. The thing to do is to practice picking up and holding the bow, then the violin, separately, a dozen times a day during the first month. For you and your child, this is more effective than one long period of practice every day. On waking, after dressing, before breakfast . . . so goes the day. Can't you see yourself getting breakfast while you practice? It only takes about 60 seconds to do the "numbers game" a couple of times. It's no fairer for you to make excuses than for your son. Get in to the spirit of the thing together.

The principles of violin playing, you'll find, are easier for you to understand than for your child. There must be *some* advantages to being older than three! You can be sure that we teachers are most amazed and delighted with what we see you young mothers accomplishing. Keep me posted.

With best wishes,

Elizabeth

Dear Sheila,

So a year has passed since Bobby began to play and you met your first challenges yourself in handling a violin? I imagine you enjoyed it thoroughly a good deal of the time, and at other times found your ingenuity tested. If Bobby is like most Suzuki students turning four, he has spent most of his first year mastering the variations to "Twinkle, Twinkle Little Star"—or perhaps I should say, mastering the techniques of handling the violin and mastering control of his body balance,

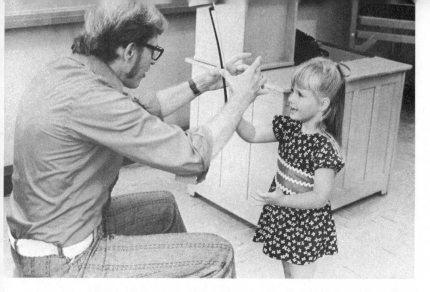

As she draws her bow through an arc provided by Theodore Brunson, a Suzuki teacher, this child shows pleasure in the development of control.

while the foundation rhythms developed in him the senses of tempo and of bowing style.

I imagine you, like most mothers starting children of three with music lessons, have run into friends who looked askance at the whole idea. They either thought you were a monster trying to prevent your child from having a normal life, or that if you really wanted a prodigy you should be turning to a more traditional approach for his foundation studies.

At times you may suffer anxieties as the mother of a Suzuki student. "Where are the scales my son should be practicing?" you may ask after you have met the mother of a student playing in the traditional way. "Where are the etudes?" Allay your fears. First, your son probably will be able to play rings around most of his more traditional counterparts. Second, he should be experiencing all of the benefits gained in the study of the scales. It is most important to extract the technical material in the arpeggios that lurk in a Bach minuet or from the repertory in the Suzuki books, which include also, technique books devoted to bowing, shifting, and double stops. Or they may be presented in capsule form as specific practice exercises coordinated with the carefully chosen standard literature in the ten Suzuki books. What are called "games" at recitals are in reality engaging exercises for the improvement of technique, as well as for alert control.

It would be nice to think that with all of this inflow— regular listening to good records, lessons from an experienced teacher, and help at home—there would be a matching outflow at all times. In theory the outflow must match the inflow, but we are dealing with humans, who can catch the inflow and store it for a long period without releasing it. It is hard to tell what a child has actually absorbed. We must, therefore, take much on faith. Don't worry about lessons that don't seem to "take." It is the total over the long haul that counts, not what your son seems to produce each week. It is common for young children to refuse to do anything that seems expected of them at a lesson and then to go home and do it all when the pressure is removed. Because many children meet strong demands from adults by acquiesing and playing more than they are

The one-to-one relationship between child and teacher is maintained in the individual lesson which forms the core of the Suzuki approach.

really ready for from within, their playing gradually takes on a mechanical sound and their facial expressions and body motions are very different from those of the child who develops more slowly but from within.

Which do you want? Choose your road carefully.

In summary, here is a program for the mother of a violin student:

Avoid making issues, even though we all know disciplined regularity is an ultimate necessity for musical achievement. What we know in theory can't always be put into practice. If your household is extremely well organized, perhaps a practice schedule will work beautifully. If you are erratic, informal, and subject to enthusiastic impulses, the practice pattern will be a different story. Don't expect your child to be essentially different in his practice habits from the total family pattern. This is not to say that you can't change the family pattern gradually as you grow together in new directions. Just don't put all the blame for a poor practice habit on the child's temperament – or the phase he is going through.

If the child recognizes some progress toward the end of each practice period it will be more likely that he will look forward to the next practice session. He may need help in finding that progress. Most children are suspicious of general remarks like, "that was very good" unless they are very tiny. Many children can hear only the negative things about their playing unless helped to balance the picture. They will believe your comments if you remark on specific improvements. The most helpful type run something like this: "Your tone is better today" or "you certainly could play that part of the piece faster than yesterday" or "you stood much taller today."

Progress can also be better noted in one of the review pieces than in the newest number. Form a pattern of ending each practice session with a favorite review piece, where success is assured. It is most important to end each practice with a good sound in the ear.

Dr. Suzuki's concept of the correct division of time in the daily musical experience is illustrated in the division of the circle below:

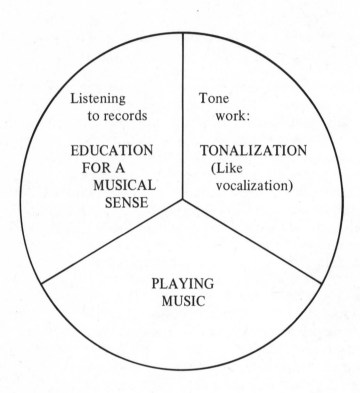

1) *Attend lessons,* except on advice of the teacher after consultation. Keep in the background while there, remembering that the child cannot learn from two teachers at once. If you handle it well, after a few weeks he will not often look your way during lessons.

2) *Help him recall the lesson.* This begins in the car after leaving the studio. It should never wait 24 hours. It will be hard enough for you to remember. Take notes yourself at lessons, though the child should still be encouraged to remember as much as he can. If you have taped the lesson on a cassette, you can replay it in the car immediately.

3) *Handle the violin yourself at home,* learning to play the first book at least.

4) *Be responsible for playing the current record daily,* helping establish the basic patterns of record use. Positive comments from you which show interest can also help train him to listen effectively. "How smoothly the tones are connected," or "I never noticed those accents before," are the type of comment most helpful.

5) *Become accustomed to repetition* of the recorded models and of continued use of the same repertoire over long periods, Remember that *children* do not tire of repetition unless others show boredom in their remarks, manner, or tone of voice. The safest way to avoid this is to form the habit of searching for new ideas overlooked previously. Not only will you keep interested, but you will help your child listen.

6) *See that the violin and bow are in good condition,* and that the teacher's recommendations for supplies or repairs are promptly taken care of. Keep in mind the following essential elements before the technique of playing can be at all effective:

    good horsehair, at proper tension (rehair bow about once yearly)

    good rosin, used daily

    good strings (not dull or false)

    properly adjusted violin (good bridge correctly fitted,

and sound post in proper position, pegs and tuners that work, and no unglued joints or cracks).

If the violin is broken and in need of glue, do not attempt home repairs. Most glue jobs involve the know-how of a regular violin repair man and are very inexpensive. Make sure the rosin is in usable shape, not in bits. Rosin the bow yourself if it looks shiny against the light. Many children don't apply enough at first, while later they apply too much. In that case, clouds of dust fly from the bow when the thumb nail is drawn across the hair near the frog. This is the frequent cause of rough, scratchy tone. Make sure the bow hair tension is correct as shown by the teacher, with care taken to relax the tension at the end of each practice. Many bow sticks are warped and ruined by failure to learn correct and regular use of the screw. Also, train your child not to touch the horsehair when resting.

7) *See that your child attends all recitals, classes and special events* since these are scheduled for motivation and musical education. The recitals are quite unique in character, and provide enjoyment for the students, the families, and many

The small group sessions which supplement the individual lessons give students a chance to learn from each other and to enjoy music together.

visitors. Show interest in other students but avoid making comparisons between your child and others. Such comparisons tend to be unfair to all concerned, especially since you know a great deal about your own child and very little about the backgrounds of the others.

8) *Keep growing*—musically, as well as in other ways. Children grow best in an atmosphere of adult growth, It is contagious.

9) *Give serious attention to Suzuki's concepts.* They are the fruits of a long life of musical and spiritual search. The children of the world may well benefit from the extension of his ideas into many fields.

10) *Avoid discouragement.* When in need of a lift, remember such statements of Suzuki's as the following:

"How we teach is not as important as how we give." (You are your child's teacher, too, so take note.)

"When love is deep, much can be accomplished."

11) *Practice with your child until he can work effectively on his own.* Two or more practice periods a day are far better than one long period, throughout one's study. Dr. Suzuki advised one mother of a three year old, "Two minutes with joy, five times a day."

If you wish to help your child achieve permanent good violin posture, plan where you sit or stand in relation to him. Try to keep to his left so that he can look directly along the strings and over the scroll at you—without spoiling his alignment. If he moves, you can move too. If you go to the piano, align him again so that he can look toward you along his normal sight line when holding the violin properly.

Accustom your child to help in fixing his fingers on the bow from time to time, to shaping his left hand over the fingerboard, and to helping him establish the violin correctly on his shoulder from time to time also. This should be continued for most of the first year, except with mature students capable of taking care in making such adjustments themselves.

Keep in mind the helpful slogan of alignment: *Nose, strings, elbow, foot (left)*.

12) *Be responsible for getting practice started,* as well as for helping your child learn how to practice. Don't blame your child for not remembering to practice, or for not wanting to stop doing something else. Don't shout out the window, "Stop your play this minute and come in to practice." Experiment with ideas from other parents. Many mothers report that children appear if they hear their mother start to practice the violin. (The *child's* pieces of course—this doesn't apply to mothers who already play violin.) Others find similar results if they start to play the current violin record. Remember, too, that nothing works forever.

Keep inventing new challenges, *a la* Suzuki. Keep him playing while you talk to him. This will help him take corrections from the teacher without having to interrupt his playing.

Remember that practice is lonely and children like company when practicing. If your child starts resenting your help, take stock of your ways. Keep a light touch, without diminishing the sense of practice being important. Remember the value of change for the sake of change. Expect ups and downs and plateaus.

Dr. Suzuki doesn't guarantee that the application of his concept will turn your child into a prodigy (for that is not his goal), although for some children it is doing so. He does say unreservedly that through it any child can learn to play beautifully, and in so doing will gain greater dignity and happiness. It is for us, as parents and humanitarians, to provide the environment in which this spiritual growth becomes possible. I wish you luck in this adventure and with all best wishes remain,

Yours sincerely,

Elizabeth

Chapter 3

The Psychology of Early Learning

Mae Ferro

"Children need time to develop, to test to explore, to repeat, to reinforce, to acquire, to learn. As parents, give children the time they need."

Learning to play the violin under the Suzuki method resembles the acquisition of other skills, whether mathematics, physics, or tennis. Reading, the highly complex skill that I teach, is not unlike violin playing. Preparation for it begins at the moment of birth, not on the first day of school. Children bring all of their past experiences and development to either process.

Since the child has been preparing for reading since birth, it is the parents who are the child's first teachers. The relationship of child to parents in both reading and musical experiences is vital to progress. Why do some children fail to read when they are of an age when society expects them to acquire the skill? One reason may be that they remain undeveloped, or at least lag behind in development of certain areas of their growth. Let's relate these areas to the Suzuki method, with its emphasis on strong child-parent learning relationships.

All that a child knows he learns, and learning begins at birth with the infant's first movement. Learning throughout life is developed from and built upon the information that he gains from his first movements, his relationship to the various objects of his world. Movement is the basis of all knowledge and intellectual performance. By moving, a child learns about, first, his own body; second, the relationship of his body to objects around him; and third, the relationship of objects to each other and to himself.

First consider what he learns about himself. He learns that he can direct the movements of his body to achieve a goal. To the infant movement is an end in itself. His hands and feet both respond to and create his moods. At this age the accomplishment of the activity itself affords satisfaction. Whoever has seen a baby throwing a toy will understand.

But the child later learns to direct the movements of his body to achieve a goal. That is, the sound of a ball bounding on a floor is a pleasant response which suggests to the child that he has a growing power. The child can stroke an object by reaching out to touch it. He learns to coordinate his hand with signals from his eyes.

Next, he learns to crawl—to move his whole body, coordinating it with the visual signals that he is learning to interpret. He can cross a room without bumping into furniture, directing his body toward a specific goal. Now movement has become not an end in itself, but a tool to accomplish his purposes. Walking is first a skill and then a tool. One learns to walk to accomplish things; and at the same time he learns to avoid hazards inherent in the process.

By the time the child has been enrolled in school his processes will have become extraordinarily sophisticated. He can move his eyes across a printed page and from the blackboard to the paper on his desk. He can hold a pencil and coordinate his muscles with his eyes while writing. His degree of success in these tasks will depend upon his earlier visual motor learning. His capacities as a scholar will rest upon the earlier development of his whole being.

The human hand is a precise and forceful instrument. It can be powerful, as when it holds a hammer to strike a nail, or finely sensitive, as when it discerns small differences in textures. The sensitivity of the hands cannot be separated from the accuracy with which they move. There is also high correlation between a child's awareness of his fingers and his ability to execute fine motor movements.

One can see how early experience with the violin can help to develop the use and awareness of the hands. The player must coordinate the fingers of one hand with his movement of the bow in the other. The violin player is especially aware of finger movements because an immediate auditory feedback tells him what he has done.

Hopefully, parents will realize the complexity of such motor skills. A young child is not ready to handle all of them with the agility of an adult. Only a few years ago psychologists would recognize a new developmental stage when the child simply executed a new gross motor movement. But think of how far beyond gross movement the young violinist must proceed. In addition to merely holding the violin correctly he must learn to make the fine movements that produce music and quality of tone. These coordinations are difficult for people of any age.

To demand that a child perform a fine motor task for which he is not developmentally ready is to invite withdrawal, rebellion, or tension; or he may placate his teacher and parents by performing the task in a rudimentary way that is of small help or comfort to him. We see the results of this strain often in children's handwriting. When a child has been forced to write before he has achieved the proper visual-motor integration he will hold the pencil in a most awkward and uncomfortable manner, making no differentiation in pattern when at the blackboard or on a piece of small paper. The handwriting is usually poor, and once such patterns and habits are established, they are difficult to correct.

His movements also teach the child that he is at the center of his own universe. Left and right, up and down, in front of and behind, all have meaning only in relation to one's own body, in the space in which the body and the objects are situated. Without some awareness of these physical relationships a person would have difficulty judging distances, shapes, and sizes. The child learns early that he can move his arms in the same or in opposite directions, or that he can move one hand and keep the other still. He learns how to balance his body, when to extend his hands, and how to catch an object. His muscles respond to the information that he gets through his eyes.

Inability to perceive the position of an object, its position in relation to one's own body, leads to severe difficulties in learning. Taking reading as one clear example, it will cause the reversal of letters such as "d" and "b," "u," and "n." It leads to confusion of words such as "saw" and "was," which are reversible, or "stop" and "spot," which differ only in sequence. The obstacle raised by this shortcoming is also present if the goal is to learn how to play the violin, which requires the coordination of bow, instrument, and body by a sensitive mind that accurately perceives all of the qualities of music.

The child's awareness of the two sides of his body is associated with a directional awareness of left to right sequence.

At an Institute session a teacher, Jeannette Scott, shows children how to gain directional sense in the control and movement of their bows.

This knowledge enables him to move his eyes from left-to-right—to follow printed words or notes, or his fingers on, strings. It is not a natural movement; it is learned, requiring fine muscle control.

Not only does the violin require that the two hands must coordinate and that the child be aware of finger movement but it increases body awareness of the position of the chin, shoulder, arms, and the location of one body part in relation to another. In his highest stage of musical development the child will feel that the violin has become a part of his body, that the slightest harmonic is sensed by the very tips of his nervous system as though it has come from inside of him rather than outside. But this knowledge is gained only by his appreciation of music and the movements that create it.

Through movement the child learns to distinguish objects from each other and their surroundings. He can, because of an astonishingly complex function of the brain, discern that a ball is coming at him from a background of trees and clouds. Later he will use this same skill to distinguish the separate letters and words on a printed page. That is, he is able to give his attention to a figure and to ignore the background. This skill is important both for seeing and for hearing, for both require that we separate appropriate stimulus from background.

This important skill of giving attention to an object without regard for its background is vital to concentration. A child who cannot black out interfering sounds, sights, feelings, or thoughts is so easily distracted from the task that he is trying to accomplish that learning is almost impossible. Young children are easily distracted, and parents of young children should be aware of the susceptibility to the confusion. If the young child is having difficulty concentrating during a music lesson everything should be done to minimize environmental distractions, whether traffic noises, siblings, or leaky faucets.

Having separated the stimuli from their background the child acquires information concerning size, shape, distance, and all other characteristics of the objects in his world. Movement and the use of all of his senses enable him to do so. He can identify objects visually only after establishing all of their individual characteristics. His senses take in the information. Through perception his brain interprets the information based on his past experiences with similar stimuli.

Whether to learn music or reading, the auditory skill is also required. To read we must learn to attach a sound to a letter, to create music, a sound to a note. Children must be able to discriminate between different sounds, to be aware of individual sounds in sentences or musical phrases. Often our manner of speaking damages comprehension. We say, "whatcha doing" as if it were one accurate word. To decode the sequence of letters in a written word the child must be aware of the sequence of sounds. He must also remember sounds and words in order to store information in the memory. This enables him to recall meaning—or music—when he hears the sound again.

The child must have a sense of temporal sequence in order to read and to spell, and his sense of rhythm is vital to his sense of timing. In his development of perception there are two fundamental dimensions—the spatial and the temporal; and they are connected by memory. Very often adults unwittingly confuse a child in his efforts to acquire a sense of time. We are not consistent and accurate in our vocabulary when we discuss time dimensions.

To read, the child must be able to see the word as a whole, break the word down into the temporal succession of sounds, and then blend the succession back to a simultaneous impression. He has to realize that the spatial order of signs represents the temporal sequence of sounds in the same word. He has to learn that the sequence of sounds and letters makes a difference and is important.

As you work with your child and his violin you will realize that a musical instrument has marvelous opportunities for developing auditory, temporal, sequential, and rhythmic skills. The child who develops them to play "Twinkle, Twinkle

Little Star" will find, upon entering school, that these same skills are needed to learn to read. As he imitates music he is exercising his auditory discrimination and his auditory memory, as well as his awareness and sense of time and rhythm. Since reading is based on language, the parent's verbal relationship with the child is a very important one in the development of reading skills. To help him to read, talk to him. Give him words and concepts. When you give a command, follow it with a reason so that he is exposed to the verbalization of cause and effect. "Johnny, please stop banging on that pot, Mommy can't hear what Daddy is saying." This is a valuable learning presentation. It is much preferred to "Stop that!" for intellectual as well as emotional, psychological, and social reasons.

This same psychology is applicable to the teaching of music. If a child is to learn to play, he must first learn to listen, to hear each note accurately. The home, surely, is the best place to help him in this process; and the most important contribution that the parent can make to it is to play and respect music himself. The parent who sends his child to music lessons but never listens to music himself, in these days of fine and inexpensive recordings, is missing an opportunity to share a pleasure with the child.

Whether dealing with reading or music, adults must eventually resort to language. They make assumptions about them because of common experiences with words, but children must be more precise. Whenever you talk about the child's violin or give him directions, be sure that he understands what you are talking about. What are the meanings of "bridge," "bow," "short side of the bridge," "pitch," "range," "scales"? Use these times as opportunities to verbalize, explore, and have fun with words. If a child has failed to follow directions, stop and think: is his reaction due to your confusing him with unclear verbalization? To be sure, ask him to restate your directions in his own words.

The relationship of the parent to the child in a learning

John Kendall, pioneer in the introduction of the Suzuki concept to the United States, explains a point to children at a Suzuki Institute.

situation should be warm, loving, and relaxed. If it isn't, the child will know it. He will quickly get the message if he is being manipulated for adult purposes. No two children are alike; each develops according to his own timetable. To use your child to play "Keep up with the Joneses," pushing him before he is ready, denies this simple truth. Yet although all children have their own rate of growth, each child follows the same pattern of development. Thus the degree of help needed by each child differs. Allow for as much repetition as your child needs. Don't rush him. You may be bored, but he isn't. Repetition is natural to intuitive learning. The child instinctively repeats to reinforce the skill. He is taking great pleasure in learning. The infant who drops his rattle repeatedly and cries to have it returned, only to drop it again, is acquiring, reinforcing, testing, and learning all kinds of important skills and concepts. His mother may be worn out, but he is working very hard, taking great delight in learning.

Learning is an exhilarating experience. Children love to learn and to work hard, happily, and naturally. If your child insists upon playing one rhythm over and over, encourage him. His intuitive learning ability will tell him when it is time for him to move on. Time is a precious gift that a parent can make. Our world is moving so fast, and we adults are so affected by this hectic pace, that we suffer from the lack of time to comprehend and take comfort from what we have learned. We must protect our young children from the same "future shock." Children need *time* to develop, to test, to explore, to repeat, to reinforce, to acquire, to learn. As parents, give children the *time* they need.

If you find yourself pushing too hard, examine your motives. Music education should be an opportunity for growth. One of Dr. Suzuki's chief goals is not to produce professionals, but to produce finer people. If you concur in this, let your expectation for your child's development be based on respect for *his* fulfillment as a person, not yours. All learning should contribute to aiding the individual to attain self-fulfillment and development of his highest potential.

Abraham Maslow, a psychologist, lists five basic needs which must be filled if the organism is to grow to its highest potential. They are given in the order of priority, that is, with respect to the order in which they are needed. The amount of energy that a child must devote to fulfilling a need at a higher level is dependent upon how much energy he devotes to fulfilling that need at a lower level. These are the needs:

1) The physiological needs—the need to avoid hunger, thirst, cold.

2) The need for safety.

3) The need for love.

Love is a very important area for children. Many do not have this need fulfilled. Children must know that they are loved: loved for themselves, exactly the way they are, not for something they should become. With the fulfillment of this need comes warmth, security, and the ability to devote energies to the next level of need.

4) The need for self-esteem.

Again, parents play a vital role in helping a child to meet this need. A strong self-image is important to all learning. A child must feel that he is important, can learn, and is worthy of being taught. Building a good self-image is essential to self-fulfillment, as modern learning theory has shown. Recent studies in language acquisition, child development, and Suzuki philosophy itself have emphasized the role of intuituve learning. A child must have confidence in himself if he is to trust his intuitive knowledge. If he thinks of himself as stupid or worthless or inferior, he will not have the security and trust to make attempts based on his inner feelings or to judge when something "feels right" to him.

5) At the highest level is self-actualization.

If all other needs have been met the child is able to devote all of his energy to achieving his fullest potential and to finding self-fulfillment. Self-actualization is the mature ability to seek and to reach deeply satisfying, useful goals. Parents want total fulfillment for their child. By satisfying the lower needs the parents can help their child to attain this highest level. But if part of the child's energies are devoted to trying to be loved and part to gaining self-esteem, he cannot have much energy left to devote to fulfillment of self-actualization.

A healthy self-image is based upon successes. Be certain that your child is given activities at which he can succeed. Failure is very damaging to self-esteem and to the ability to learn. Following the Suzuki principle, allow a child to experience success, avoiding negative criticism. Challenging a child is good for learning, but be sure that the challenge follows successes and that it is within the limits of the child's ability to respond.

Respect is the most important element in the relationship between parent and child. Sincere love for your child, loving him as he is, establishing an environment of approval and respect for him, will set a firm ground for learning. Luckily for humanity, a child's first teachers are his parents—the people who are most likely to love and respect him.

Chapter 4

Teaching Suzuki Book I

Marian Schreiber

"Each piece builds upon and assists in the development of technique in the others."

Hints and Suggestions

The progress and development of a child depends in large measure upon the teacher's understanding and presentation of the material in the first volume. In these earliest beginnings we must form a secure foundation upon which all later technique rests.

At group sessions children attentively listen to each other play solos, awaiting their turn to demonstrate what they have learned.

SUZUKI CONCEPT

I have divided Book I into three levels.

Level One consists of the first five pieces—"Twinkle, Twinkle Little Star" through "O Come Little Children."

Level Two—"May Song" through and including "Andantino."

Level Three—Bach "Minuet Nos. 1, 2, and 3."

Gavotte by Gossec is a bridge into Book II. On that bridge we return again and again to this piece and the others of Book I. According to Dr. Suzuki's own words, "By this means, while new pieces are added, emphasis is laid on increasing the ability to play the pieces already learned, thus increasing little by little the performing skill." In and between each level a strong preparation period is necessary so the problems of each new level can be dealt with successfully.

LEVEL ONE

The same attention must be given to the fundamental "STOP FORM." Dr. Suzuki refers to "STOP FORM" as the separated tones. These strokes are used within the "square" of the bow arm and indicated on the stick by means of a marked tape. A beginning student will experience difficulty in stopping on the string, and usually with a characteristically "crunchy" noise. Gradual elimination of this problem will occur with a teacher's diligence and repeated reminders to make the string echo as it does after pizzicato. (Demonstrate the plucked sound.)

Before playing any piece, *preparation* is of the utmost importance. Preparing of the position includes correct body posture, bow on the string and left hand preparation of fingers 1, 2, & 3 on "A" string. The "preparation" habit, if well developed at the beginning, will shape the hand and train the fingers to find their places on the fingerboard tapes. Tapes are later eliminated when the hand is formed and the ear developed to adjust to pitch.

Accustom the child to the terminology used. For example,

"open the string" means the formed fingers lift from the string, poised above the string with all the finger pads "looking down" at the string just released. The bow hair sets on the string—horse hair touching—only please don't press.

I. *Twinkle, Twinkle Little Star* - (Arranged by Dr. Suzuki)

1) Ideally all the rhythms should be mastered to some degree on the open strings before attempts are made to use fingers. Games can be made with each hand individually before playing together.

2) The A Major Scale is then taught using the 3 fingers on A and follow the same pattern on E.

3) Teach the child and mother how to practice. Show them how to think each tone and finger position before playing.

4) Caution the child's mother to note the change of arm level for A string and that of E string posture.

5) "Stop Form," changing the string, and then proceeding to a new string level is essential training in the early stages. This problem renews itself continually throughout study. As a consequence, much progress will be made through proper changing of bow levels.

6) The teacher must exercise extreme care in teaching the blocked finger position. Finger independence, flexibility and suppleness must never be sacrificed. Some children learn to place all three fingers simultaneously on A string for the "Twinkles" and then the need develops to unlearn this crippling habit.

7) The theme of "Twinkle" poses a new concept of lengthened tones, yet still contained within the marked tape of the bow. The separated sounds remain, but travel———slowly for the half note! In recent years the Japanese have become accustomed to using the whole bow for the theme.

II. *Lightly Row* - Folk Song

1) The bowing begins on E string—note E string bowing posture.

2) In the beginning "prepare" 1st and 2nd finger—then "open the string." Now practice the placement of 2nd finger only (the shape of the other fingers remains over the finger-board). Begin early to establish finger independence in this manner.

3) The bowing of separate tones is similar to the theme of Twinkle, perhaps allowing slightly more stroke than the tape markings.

4) In order to make music from the start I like to teach the meaning of *ritardando* to the child and demonstrate this within the final three notes of the music—♩ ♩ (pause) ♩ (slowly.)

III. *Song of the Wind* - Folk Song

Before a child begins this piece, or for that matter any of the following pieces, it is a wise plan to select the new idea contained therein which needs additional practice.

1) "Song of the Wind" presents three new concepts.

    a) Measure three contains the first string crossing with first finger remaining on "E" while the 3rd finger moves horizontally from "A" to "E" then back again to the already positioned 1st finger.

    b) Lifting the bow—to reset again for the new down stroke.

    c) Repeat sign.

2) Show the child with his mother the "special spots" that must be worked out carefully in the music. Draw the child over to the open music page and point out these important places. While they are not reading at this time, they will learn much from the signs and markings indicated. Eventually they will watch for these places as they listen to their recordings, following the score with their fingers!

3) Refer to (1) above.

Making a game of keeping 1st finger on "E" string, alternate with 3rd finger "A" to 3rd finger "E" string saying:

    "Walk-ing, walk-ing cross the track,

    Rail-road train is com-ing back."

(Pluck "A" string and sing "Toot.")

Some children enjoy such games as the above which give them pleasure in verse while assisting in the otherwise awkward horizontal motion one might be inclined to neglect.

4) Refer to (3) above.

Practice the lifted bow using "bow balance" exercise above the string. Try counting to four—on count one and two play "E" string within the bow tape— on counts three stop on the string—on count four lift the bow and reset to begin again. Repeat this exercise many times. Set the bow horse hair down gently—silently, so the bow will not bounce or scratch. Measure ten is "Quickly set"—take care—there is no rest here for time out.

5) Point out the similarity of the first two measures of this music to the third and fourth measures of "Lightly Row."

IV. *Go Tell Aunt Rhody* - Folk Song

Because my students are privileged to be studying the Kodaly method they are familiar with ♩ ♫♩ ♩ ♩
ta ti ti ta ta

1) The children clap, singing ♩ ♫♩ ♩ ♩ etc.
ta ti ti ta ta

2) Follow the music score with fingers while singing *ta ti ti ta ta,* etc.

3) Listen to the record try to sing the *ta's* and *ti ti's* on the correct rhythm.

4) Before playing, take only the bow and draw a half-way mark on the tape. Explain that now all the ♩ notes including
ta
half notes will still use only the length of the bow tape, but the ♫ uses only half of the tape. This controlled use of
ti ti
only the upper half of the tape requires extreme concentration and attention.

5) Practice moving the left hand finger along the tape on the bow while singing *ta ti ti ta ta.* Alternate with a quiet finger while the bow moves along the finger to the rhythm.

6) This piece begins like "Lightly Row" with the 2nd finger on "A" string. Unlike "Lightly Row" the bowing starts on "A" string.

7) When playing bow and fingers together, measure three requires a quick change of string. Make exercises here for string crossing.

8) Teach now the terms *forte* and *piano* with their meaning. Measure 5 and 6 are played *forte*. Use a little more than the bow's tape to produce the forte sound, *Piano* is soft; use a little less of the bow's tape to make soft sound.

9) Demonstrate how to shape the phrase at the conclusion of this piece.

10) In the beginning separated tones can be used on all the quarter notes so a clear clean tone may be maintained. At a later time a more *legato* sound can be taught.

Begin at this point to teach a longer bow stroke. Experiment with the theme of Twinkle or the A Major scale using more bow. Separated tones are still used so each sound has a beautiful start and ending. The same good quality and volume of sound must remain from beginning to end of each stroke.

Explain now about *Tonalization*. Emphasis must be placed on the *daily practice* of exercises given in the book to develop beautiful tones.

V. *O Come Little Children*

1) Up bow for the first time. The bow remains on the string. Use elbow to initiate up bow stroke.

2) Teach repeat with 1st and 2nd endings.

3) Teach the meaning of *crescendo* and *diminuendo* and demonstrate their use in this piece.

In the first learning require the child to limit the bow to the same short bows. After both the melody and correct bowing have been mastered, teach *crescendo* and *diminuendo*. *Crescendo* begins after the second ending, reaching a climax in the last three measures, followed by *diminuendo* to the conclusion.

LEVEL TWO

VI. *May Song*

1) Rhythmic difficulty: ♩. ♪ Use small bow for the eighth note.

2) Measure three has a quick change of string. Take care to make a beautiful sound on the open string.

3) Try for musical feeling in this piece which uses more bow throughout. However, the ♫ pattern is still "tiny bow."

4) Make a special point of the 3rd finger A in the opening measure. This important up bow stroke is the same as the climax of "O Come, Little Children" in the previous piece— Similar also the E string tonalization exercise (Tonalization page 13).

5) This piece concludes on A and begins again on A making the repeat another difficulty.

6) Measure five and six—play *forte*. Measure seven and eight—play *piano*.

I continue to use these technique builders from an earlier Zen-On edition. Finger-patterns need to be used.

VII. *Long Long Ago* - Bayly

1) This is the first experience with the 1st finger on the "D" string. Prepare the "D" string.

The original Suzuki violin edition included certain special finger exercises at each of the LEVELS indicated above. I continue to use the following technique builders throughout:

2) Teach contrast, *forte* and *piano,* in measures 9 & 10, 11 & 12.

3) Show about phrasing: use *crescendo—diminuendo.*

4) This is an excellent piece for the children to play expressively and become involved within the music.

5) Be careful not to cheat on the rhythm of the sustained half notes.

6) Measure eight involves a lifted bow to the frog for the *forte* passage.

VIII. *Allegro* - Suzuki

1) Separated tones but not *staccato.*

2) Teach *ritardando,* and *fermata* ⌒ , *a tempo* and *dolce.*

3) Previous preparation of the second measure is important. Some children experience difficulty with finger and bow coordination. In measure two, the rhythmic pattern is the same as "Twinkle," ♫♫♩ but with a slower tempo with different note values.

Have the child bow ♫♫♩ ♩ while the teacher places 1st finger on E string. When the rhythm is well established surprise the student with playing of the fingers. Later reverse; teacher bows and the child fingers. Make up finger exercises for quick and correct movement of fingers on the string.

4) Dr. Suzuki has his advancing students return again and again to this piece to teach upper arm bow movement with whole arm involvement.

5) The first tone is a "key" tone and was emphasized in tonalization studies as well as in pieces (V) and (VI). The bowing now begins near the frog and on down bow.

IX. *Perpetual Motion* - Suzuki

1) Notice a return again to the small bows at the marked portion of tape on the bow.

2) Begin with tiny bows with each stroke the same size.

3) Use separate tones: practice slowly at first, then gradually speed the tempo. (Teacher watches for relaxed bow arm but with a firm bow grip so the tip is controlled.)

4) The open E string is used to allow practice for quick changing of strings (watch elbow).

5) When the eighth notes have been mastered, add the sixteenth note variation.

FOURTH FINGER EXERCISE (Book 1, Page 16.)

1) Presentation of the 4th finger. Mark fingerboard with a tape for the 4th finger.

2) Play open string and then 4th finger. Draw attention to the same pitch, although, a slightly different quality.

3) *Listen* for the resonance of the E string as the 4th finger plays on the A string. *See* the E string vibrate as the 4th finger plays on A string.

Explain about tonalization for the 4th finger. Teach the child to both *see* and *hear* the resonant sound.

4) It is a basic principle to leave the 1st finger on the string in this exercise while moving to open string or remaining on the same string.

5) Use a slow tempo in the beginning, playing with separated tones.

6) 1st finger intonation must be perfect.

After teaching the D Major tonalization study and the D Major scale, I teach the simple D string finger exercise formerly used in the Japanese editions.

Teach "Perpetual Motion" in D Major; play D Major scale with the "Twinkle" rhythms.

Show the arm and bow levels on these two new strings.

Practice "Perpetual Motion" also on the G string.

Teach the one octave G Major scale with the corresponding finger exercise on the G string.

X. *Allegretto* - Suzuki

1) Practice the new rhythm on the open D string. This new rhythm is the reverse pattern of the "Twinkle" rhythm ♪♪♫ ♪♪♫ ; *Allegretto* ♫♪ ♩ ♫♪ ♩.

2) Practice the new rhythm on the D Major scale.

3) The child experiences the flow of the music and phrasing as the teacher demonstrates.

4) Use open strings rather than the newly taught 4th finger at first so the ability to quickly change strings with clarity can be established.

5) Practice this music lightly: tempo more quickly.

6) The middle section is played more *legato*.

7) Measure nine: Practice 1st finger movement from D string to G string. Use "Stop form" while the finger finds the correct place.

8) Observe the *ritardando, fermata* ⌢, and *a tempo*.

XI. *Andantino* - Suzuki

1) Clap the rhythm. Observe the similarity of pattern groups with "Allegretto" but note the different rhythmic emphasis.

2) Teach accents on the half note.   Accents are made here by the speed of the bow. Do not press.

3) Show gradually how to read and recognize signs in music. Arouse the child's interest in reading.

4) (a) *ritardando*
   (b) *a tempo*
   (c) *fermata*—count 1, 2, then proceed.

At this crucial level we need to prepare for a new pattern of finger placement and sound.

The following exercises from the original edition are most advantageous in introducing the close 1−2 position. They also serve as an introduction to the slur, both in *staccato* and *legato* passages.

SUZUKI CONCEPT

Teach also the G Major scale, two octaves.
1) Ascending, use open string
2) Descending, use 4th finger
3) Use the different "Twinkle" rhythms and various note values.
4) Use as a tonalization exercise.

Accustom the children to practice their *"Daily Dozen"* each day. These exercises can be made up at the discretion of the teacher and adapted to the individual needs of the student, including tonalization, finger exercises, scales, bow or left hand development.

XII. *Etude* - Suzuki

1) Same as "Perpetual Motion" but the first time all four strings are used within one piece.
2) Point out the G Major scale in the music.
3) If possible, leave the 1st finger down where indicated.
4) Separate tones are important.
5) Teaching how to change string levels is essential.
6) Call attention to measures 8 & 9 where the opening phrase of Bach Minuet #2 is introduced. Give extra care and attention to this G Major passage which, if well learned, reaps benefits in the Bach Minuet.

LEVEL THREE

The folk tunes and melodies of the repertoire in the above levels are charming and melodious. In Level Three we arrive at solid musical material by the greatest of composers, Bach. The children should have acquired certain skills in the previous material so the playing of these compositions will produce a new quality of musical maturity in performance. With careful teaching and mastery of the preliminary steps, the learning of the Minuets need not become a struggle, rather a pleasure in the achievement of new goals.

XIII. *Minuet No. 1* - Bach

1) The slur is introduced in the repertoire for the first time.
2) *Example A* (refer below)
   a. Practice the first measure for proper bow division and evenness of tone quality.
   b. Listen for resonant sound of this first note—strive to hear the tonalization qualities within every third finger sound in this music.
3) *Example B* (below)
   a. Use "Stop Form" to prepare string crossing to E string.
   b. Use open E for bow arm string crossing.
   c. Use 4th finger later for finger crossing.
   d. Note preparation of bow and finger at the critical points indicated.
4) *Example C* (below)
   a. Note the identical rhythmic pattern in Example C.
   b. Extra practice should be given the 3rd and 4th fingers.
   c. Careful intonation of the lowered 2nd finger.
5) *Example D* (below)
   a. Finger pattern change.
   b. A careful explanation must be presented to parent and child concerning this problem.
6) *Example E* (below)
   a. A dynamic change can be executed by the more advanced student.
7) *Example F* (below)
   a. The sustained tone must be held to the count of three and then the lifted bow reset for the repeat.
   b. Ritard. *Only* at the *very end* of the piece.

SUZUKI CONCEPT

XIV. *Minuet #2* - Bach

1) Prepare the left hand position and practice the preliminary exercise. (below)

2) Keep first finger down if possible.

3) *Example A*
   a. "Stop Form" is necessary so the child has time to think and prepare before playing.
   b. Prepare both fingers and bow for string crossings. Watch bow arm levels.

4) *Example B*
   a. Take care to prepare the interval of the 4th. Good intonation please.

5) *Examples C and D*

   a. Additional practice on string crossing is necessary.

   b. Hear the perfect octave intonation.

   c. Make resonant sound on the two up bow strokes, similar to opening in Bach Minuet #1.

6) *Example E*

   a. Introduction of D#, presenting a new finger position.

   b. Make an exercise using the close 3–4 pattern. While this rhythmic pattern is the same as Example D the finger difficulties pose problems of coordination and intonation.

   c. Demonstrate for the child and parent the new finger movement in the extended third finger position of D#.

7) *Example F*

   a. Use a small amount of bow.

   b. Prepare for string crossing.

   c. Play gently on the third beat. Remember this is a Minuet.

8) Always make the repeats. Lifted bows must be reset without a sound.

XV. *Minuet #3* - Bach

1) The problem of slurs must be given careful consideration. Point out the similarity of bowing patterns occurring throughout this piece.

2) *Example A*
  a. The appoggiatura is played in the manner indicated below.

3) *Example B*
  a. Prepare both finger and bow for all string crossings.
  b. Note arm level for different string postures.

4) *Example C*
  a. Take care to place 4th finger correctly. Practice also with a prepared lowered 2nd finger.
  b. Make exercises to strengthen fingers and increase ability to place the fingers accurately.

5) *Example D*
  a. Following a difficult sequence of bowing and finger patterns, the 2nd finger reappears in a raised position.

6) *Example E*
  a. Note the combination of problems in bowing, rhythm, and intonation.

7) *Example F*
  a. Lift the 3rd finger and reset on the D string for the perfect fifth interval crossing.
  b. Measure two: 4th finger preferred—note careful string crossing from 3rd finger D string to the 4th finger A string.

8) *Example G*
   a. Strive for good musical feeling in the playing of the
   pattern easing into the phrase ending.
9) Always make the repeats. Lifted bows must be reset
without a sound.

XVI. *The Happy Farmer* - Schumann

1) This is only the second time in the repertoire that a piece begins with up bow.

2) Practice the ♩.♪♩.♪ rhythm on the open strings. Also play "Twinkle" with this same rhythm.

3) The eighth note pattern groups are usually played on the string.

4) This piece will be a happy, fun type composition for the child who has achieved good tone, and clear, concise bowing.

5) Insist on good steady rhythm throughout.

    a. Again, the ♩.♪ rhythm must be well established.

    b. Listen for the accompaniment against the ♩.♪ violin solo part.

    c. Feel the pulse of the beat inside yourselves.

XVII. *Gavotte* – Gossec

1) The eighth note groups are played on the string, below the middle, in the lower half of the bow.

2) Upper arm involvement is important here.

3) Practice the grace note exercises (page 23, Book I).

4) *Example A*

    a. Practice separate tones first, later slurred bowings.

    b. Stop and prepare 4th finger—lift 2nd finger to reset at C4 in the lowered finger position.

5) *Example B*

    a. String crossings require much preparation for the quicker tempo.

    b. Practice slowly.

6) *Example C*

    a. Examples of similar string crossing patterns are numerous throughout this piece. Use *tiny bows.*

7) *Example D*

    a. Be careful of intonation in the interval of the fourth at the slurred string crossing.

8) *Example E*

   a. Arm levels are important here.

   b. Watch for posture on the different strings.

   c. Use "Stop Form."

9) *Example F*

   a. Observe the change in the bowing. Use the two up bows on the last *arco* strokes before pizzicato.

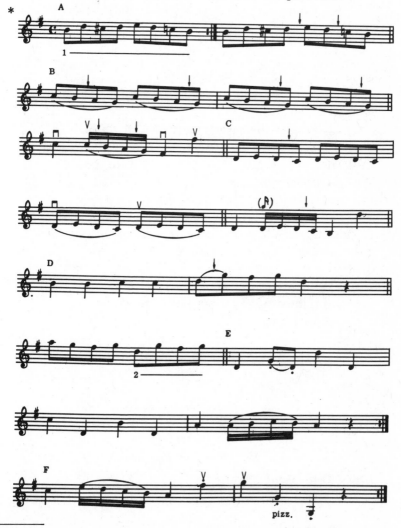

The seventeen pieces of the repertoire, Book I, have been collected, assembled and arranged in a masterly sequence. Each piece builds upon and assists the development of technique in the others. As each new step is presented and mastered, the groundwork is prepared for further advancement and progress.

Each teacher must analyze the material carefully and study ways to impart this knowledge successfully to parents and children.

Dr. Suzuki reminds us that "The way to acquire ability is to practice what one can do repetitively until it becomes a part of oneself. Ability develops from the initial ability that one can do something and is enhanced into still higher ability by practice. Ability is enhanced by ability."

He further states that "Education" in Japanese as drawn, is a combination of the characters which mean "teach" and "cultivate." In education of the mother tongue, this "cultivate" side is very much emphasized and so, excellent ability develops in every child. But recently in school education in other fields this "cultivate" portion is neglected because of the misunderstanding that education is just teaching without cultivation, and this is producing many failures in education. Though many teachers use the word "education" they are forgetting to "cultivate" ability.

We, too, must examine ourselves—determine our contribution as teachers toward this "cultivation side" of education. Let us continue our dedication with teachers all over the world "for the welfare and happiness of all children!"

Everybody has a soul. Dr. Suzuki is trying to help people realize that they have one.

A Mother

Chapter 5

Motivation

American Suzuki Institute—West

"Whatever students do well, however well, is a step in the right direction. It will deserve your honest praise."

One Japanese mother spends three-and-a-half hours a day with her two children as they study the violin. At concerts she always sits in the front row, smiling and moving with the music, bowing with her daughter as she plays. She always smiles at the lessons, too, and looks as though she enjoys every minute of it. Her children like to practice. She makes it fun. Naturally, these children have made very rapid progress.

This is motivation. Many Japanese mothers are particularly skillful in providing it. They do so because of their deep interest in their children's musical development. When listening, they give their full attention, rarely engaging in any other activity like letter-writing or needlepoint, or reading magazines. Their attitude is, "We are students, too." This strengthens their ability to help their children.

Some mothers compel their children to practice; others withdraw completely. Neither attitude will be as successful, in the long run, as the one adopted by that smiling Japanese mother, who participates with pleasure in her children's experience. Parents often turn Dr. Suzuki's advice, "Don't force your child to practice; don't make it an unpleasant experience," into a negative rather than a positive element of motivation. One parent said, "I have gotten to the point where I let my child come and tell me when he wants to practice."

I thought: "If everyone did this we would have few musicians." Most children will not practice spontaneously. It is for parents and teachers to cause them to *want* to practice. Helping to create an inner drive is not compulsion; it is motivation. We don't ask students, "Would you like to go to school today?" Nor do we allow them to choose whether or not to eat or to take care of their bodies. One important function of parents and teachers is to guide children into the proper performance of these responsibilities.

Dr. Suzuki's words were intended to prevent the forced practice that many parents impose. Pressure on a student is particularly ineffective when the student has reached the age of rebellion against authority. Practicing should be pleasant so that the child will enjoy it sufficiently to practice another time.

The Suzuki method contains within it many of the keys to motivation. One of these keys, in my opinion, is the standardized repertoire. In many cases a child will want to play a piece four or five pages ahead in his book and work all the harder to reach that point. Another key is that in the Suzuki method, students listen to each others' lessons, and parents, too, are made a part of the audience in both practice sessions and workshops. The method enables fathers to participate in the child's music education. In the ideal environment, whole families plan performances and attend concerts together, reinforcing each others' interest in the development of their musical abilities.

After each performance praise should be given—but only where it is deserved. There is always something praiseworthy in any performance. You can say, "Good, you have finished the piece." Or, "My, your posture was good in that piece." Pick something that you can honestly call "Good!" Psychologists say that this is important in working with adults, too. Before correcting someone or offering criticism, first find something to praise. Then you can go on from there, and constructive criticism will be accepted all the more readily.

The effectiveness of honest praise was shown by Dr. Suzuki's book, "Nurtured by Love." In it he describes a teacher who was completely discouraged by the failure of one of his students to play well. After hearing the boy, Dr. Suzuki thought for a moment and then said: "Good! You can play. Now can you do this?"

Intrigued, the boy said, "Yes." Then he tried to imitate Dr. Suzuki.

"Now can you do this?"

Again the boy imitated. They went on this way through a whole lesson, with the boy trying one thing after another. When it was over the teacher complimented Dr. Suzuki for giving a wonderful lesson.

"But how could you say to him, 'Good, you can play,' when his playing was so awful?" he asked.

Dr. Suzuki replied: "I didn't say, 'You can play *well*.' Some students are shy and don't want to play for me. But he played, so I gave him credit for that, and then we were able to go on and start learning."

There are many other ways to assist a child as he struggles towards perfection. Some are very simple, such as going on stage with children to make sure that they are comfortable before a performance. This gives them confidence. Another is to help them work together, avoiding strenuous competition. In Japan even very advanced players are not entered into contests until they have gained a professional polish. Although younger students would often make star performers, they are not pressed in that direction. "The only competition a child should have is with himself," Dr. Suzuki said. "Is he doing as well as he can, or is he sitting back and not developing his full potential?"

Most competitive spirit arises from mothers rather than from the children. If a mother is too competitive it might be wise to teach the child without her. The pressure which says, "Move along faster before you really learn what you are doing" is totally destructive of the learning process. Even teachers are guilty of it; they often want to show all of their knowledge at once; they point out all of the things that should be improved without realizing that they are overloading the student with criticism.

Whatever students do well, however small, is a step in the right direction. It will deserve your honest praise. As Dr. Suzuki said: "Westerners are too eager to set goals in the far-off future. They want to study to become great artists or are working too hard to win a particular competition. It is always a goal in the future instead of getting enjoyment from music as an essential part of one's daily life.

The problem of motivation is also subtle when the duration of practice is considered. When parents ask me how long their children should practice I never say—as apparently some teachers do—"Only 15 minutes a day." The only guidance I give them, especially if their question involves small children, is "It's better to practice five times a day for two minutes with preparation and good attention than it is to stick with them for half an hour when they are balking. Dr. Suzuki's expression for this is "Two minutes with joy five times a day."

Even with older children, the joy should remain as the length of time grows longer in succeeding practice sessions. When you see that a young child in a group is not concentrating you can help him to retain this pleasure in his music. Say to him, "Why don't you sit down for a while and I will teach someone else. Then I will come back to you." You will have saved him from an experience that might have dampened his motivation to play. Furthermore, you can work with him several times during a lesson, gaining his complete concentration each time.

According to Dr. Suzuki, when children can play all four variations of "Twinkle" they have already built up four minutes of concentration. At first, however, getting them through one variation is about their limit, and sometimes with small children it is best to strive for excellent tone in only one phrase. Failing this, the child may go through the motions of playing without really concentrating.

To sum up, some of the keys of motivation are:

1) Honest and joyful participation in the music by the parents and fellow students.

2) Praise for whatever the student truly does well, followed by

3) Constructive criticism when it is needed,

4) Warm support in situations of anxiety, and

5) Building self-esteem by helping the students to learn each stage completely, refusing to respond to competitive pressures.

Suzuki children are not separated by age. If they share the repertory they are encouraged to play together and to help one another.

Chapter 6

Left-Hand Techniques

Louise Behrend and Anastasia Jempelis

"... the main problem with most intonation is ... we don't hear our target."

Louise Behrend: Dr. Suzuki believes in a very firm left hand position—that is, a very firm hold on the shoulder. He even advocates slightly raising the left shoulder to hold the violin. He emphasizes the 45-degree hold rather than the flat one, both to project the tone more directly and to encourage the lower bow arm position. With this angle, almost invariably a shoulder pad will be needed. (A flat position is less likely to require a pad.)

Dr. Suzuki, positioning from the third finger, insists on quick placement of the three fingers to prepare for the descending scale in "Twinkle." The reason, I think, is a valid one, since he is working with very small children whose fingers are weak.

The turning of the hand, which is extreme with the Japanese violinists later, isn't that extreme in the beginning. That is, turning the knuckles so that the little finger base knuckle is closer to the fingerboard. This frees the first finger knuckle. "Later" is when a child begins to use his fourth finger and the rest of his left hand fluently. It even happens to some extent as they start getting down to the G and D strings. They not only bring the hand around more but, of course, there is much more movement of the elbow, as compared with the original straight line down through "nose, strings, elbow, and foot."

68

Anastasia Jempelis: One of the first points Dr. Suzuki made, when he came to our *Project Super* to train us in his approach, was to put finger placement tapes on the instrument. You put the tapes across the fingerboard, making them as thin as possible. I notice some little violins here have them too wide. We use a pencil and lay it across the string to make the tones, adjusting it to the desired pitch. We usually just put the first and third finger tapes down, since the concept of the fingers touching for half steps is so important. If the child sees two tapes which are close but not touching, he will forget that *his fingers should* touch.

Louise Behrend: Working with children at these Institutes, I've seen violins taped from "yea to nay." This is not the point. The point of the tapes that a lot of people miss is to assist in the positioning of the hand. Tapes are not infallible frets. Once the hand is secure in its positioning and not wandering all over the place or rocking about, one takes the tapes off even though intonation might not yet be 100 per cent secure. Also found helpful is the placing of a thumb tape. Those round felt circles—self-sticking ones to protect furniture—may be placed where you want the thumb tip in the beginning, at least to see if that spot works with a particular hand. It helps avoid the wrist collapse, especially if the thumb stands up, looking at the ceiling. I often put two "eyes" on the tip of the thumb with a felt-tip pen so the thumb can "look at the ceiling," at least with very young students.

All of this, as you know, is to help the child establish a good, and flexible left hand position so that he is in a position to start playing. Often you find people who are just horrified at the thought of putting anything on the fingerboard as a guide, which is why I brought it up right in the beginning. These are not to define intonation pure and simple.

To help a child with intonation, say, "Can you sing the sound in your head? Sing it in your head." You will have discovered that the main problem with most intonation is in the target practice we use for intonation work, because that's the way we play out of tune. We don't hear our target. After the note is out of tune it's too late. You must have your aural target before you play in tune at any level. Dr. Suzuki starts right away with the small children with this concept. He will play the passage in question and then say, "Sing it," and he'll stop and have the child quietly sing it. "Now play it," and miraculously it is in tune. The whole process of playing in tune is to set the mental image. Then your finger will follow. Don't try to make them sing it out loud because they may not have good vocal coordination. But they can sing in their heads.

The sooner we get the concept across of lifting with energy and spring, the faster we begin to develop a viable finger action. Dr. Suzuki speaks always of a fast finger action even in a slow tempo. Even when children are playing slowly, he insists that the action be fast. There should be quick finger placement at the beginning of the pauses to prepare the bow, which may move rapidly as in the first variation rhythm. It has a tremendous effect on finger clarity later on. Of course, it helps the cleanliness of playing and the coordination between bow and fingers.

Once I have children with a nice curved left hand position, I start what I call finger bouncing. I like to think of people having a bouncy feeling of the finger and not a flabby, flaccid feeling, or a bangy feeling. You want the spring, the bounce. I don't know what they call it in Japan but I saw it done in two ways. First, the child's hand was curved over the fingerboard while the teacher manipulated the fingers. The fingers curved and hovered, the teacher moved the fingers for the child, up and down, not being too precise about pitch placement. Just exercised them. The children then like to do it themselves. Even two-and three-year-olds will do it.

The second way consists of placing each finger down (just three fingers for little hands) and then starting with a lift motion. As you know, the lift is the hard part of any finger action, and the sooner we get the concept across of lifting with energy and spring, the faster we begin to develop a viable finger action.

Anastasia Jempelis: Many times a child will slap a finger down across two or three strings at a time. He has no concept of what string he is on. The sooner you start the concept of the finger on one string at a time, with very springy action, the better. This is a sample of what we mean by a small but important learning step.

Louise Behrend: To teach the positions, Dr. Suzuki uses one basic exercise: it is used for all the positions and played on each string in sequence as a stepwise position study. The shift is always the same; it is the 1-1 shift we use in scale passages so often. Dr. Suzuki recommends that the shift be made in a detached way, with a slight stop after each note; the shift is made smoothly but deliberately. The exercise should be played very slowly at first. Only after the student feels very secure in shifting should it be played quickly.

Although the exercise is a simple one, it contains one complication. The shift up is made legato, but the bow stops every time you shift back. The finger should be kept down in making the shift back; if it is not, the open strings are heard.

The second step in this exercise is the elimination of the eighth-note figure which results then in the following:

The student is doing basically what might be called the classical shift, that is, using the finger with which he last played to arrive in the new position. That is what this exercise is for.

Anastasia Jempelis: In the exercises it is very clear that the second eighth-note then becomes a help-note. Eventually it is supposed to be eliminated in the shift. The procedure of shifting is *still from first finger to first finger,* but the notes are played as above.

With the exception of the above, Dr. Suzuki does not give any other explanation of how to shift, nor is there any explanation in the books. (All references to Suzuki Books are to the Summy-Birchard 1970 Revised Editions.)

Louise Behrend: The same pattern is used for all the positions. In order to get used to playing within the framework of a given position, Dr. Suzuki suggests "Perpetual Motion" in that position. In the revised edition of the *Suzuki Violin School,* Dr. Suzuki introduces the position studies gradually in Books IV, V and VI.

These position exercises are what Dr. Suzuki uses in lieu of those thousands of exercises in Sevcik and in other method books. Dr. Suzuki also uses what he calls a "Position Game"; this is given on page 22 of Book IV of the Summy-Birchard revised edition. The exercises are simple; the pattern may be applied to all the positions and the same procedure of finding the note accurately should be followed in all positions.

This exercise should be done in all the positions so that you play as securely in the higher positions as you do in the first. The same procedure for finding the note accurately may be followed in working out positions in pieces and concertos. For example, in the Vivaldi A-Minor Concerto, practice over and over trying to locate the opening notes accurately in the third position, dropping the left arm to the side and bringing it up again. Finding the note accurately each time is the object of such drill.

When I first introduce the positions I use the displaced finger technique and find it one of the surest ways of locating the new position accurately:

I have never yet trained a student in the Suzuki concept of position technique who developed a fear of positions. They are absolutely fearless about wandering up and down the violin.

The next point is not Dr. Suzuki's approach, but I start position work by teaching harmonics, playing harmonics where they occur in the natural places all over the violin. The student has complete freedom when he finds his way around in the higher positions this way. I introduce this type of exercise long before I think about playing or introducing any of the position studies. You do not want your students ever to become "First position-bound." The Suzuki materials include three-and-a-half books of music in the first position. Many teachers, however, do introduce the positions before that time. In fact, I use the third position in several places in Dvorak's "Humoresque," for example, in these two places:

(measure 9)

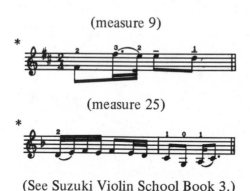

(measure 25)

(See Suzuki Violin School Book 3.)

I find that if you just show the children what to do, just say "Use these fingerings," they do it and like it.

When you go back over pieces in review (which is part of this approach), you can use the vibrato, or play them in the new positions; you can also have them use their own fingerings in the pieces.

Anastasia Jempelis: Dr. Suzuki starts doing that with the "Lullabies" for Tonalization in Book IV (page 12, violin part).

Louise Behrend: Now, going back to the problem of the shift down or back. In shifting down, do not lift the finger; even though the slide back may not be with a slur on the bow; the concept of sliding the fingers and not lifting them up and jumping back is important.

This is all that Dr. Suzuki teaches in regard to shifting but he insists that the student stay on each one of the position studies, on one string even, for some time, until it is well under control.

Question: When do you introduce the Position Etudes?

Louise Behrend: I introduce the Position Etudes at about the same time in the student's development that Suzuki does (along with the Seitz Concertos). As I mentioned previously, I start the student moving in harmonics; he finds the natural harmonics where they occur on the violin and shifts to these. I use this exercise for tonalization also. I start the student playing the harmonic on the E-string with the fourth finger. I saw a very good teacher doing this when I was in Japan; he had even first-year students tonalizing on this fourth-finger harmonic on the E-string. This particular harmonic is good because the fourth finger has to be set down accurately to produce the true harmonic.

Anastasia Jempelis: George Perlman's *Fun with a Fiddle* used harmonics for the beginner.

Louise Behrend: There is absolutely no reason why you can't. The students can always do it. The procedure is this: put the fourth finger lightly on the note B on the E string; play long, firm bows slowly, raising the bow in between each note. Try to get the feeling of the sound and the feeling of the fourth finger. Do it then in the third position, extending the fourth finger to play the harmonic. Then play harmonic sounds even up higher. I tell the students to try to find all the harmonics they can and to do their tonalization exercises on them. If the child is at least 5 or 6 years old, I am inclined to do this with that age student within the first 6 months of study. I start this *preliminary* position work by then.

I do not follow Dr. Suzuki literally in teaching scales. He teaches a few, but I teach them all. I teach them all in the first position first, just by pattern: the three open-string scales, then the first finger scale, the first finger flat scale, second finger scale, etc. I cover them all that way in pattern; I do this in one octave first. After I do this in one octave, I start the two-octave scales: G, A-flat, A, B-flat, B. Then I give the D-major scale, changing at the end of the first octave to third position. Here I use a finger substitution, replacing the third finger by the first finger on the upper note, D, as follows:

I start finger-substitute games very early, perhaps in the first year of study. However, a three- or four-year-old child is not secure enough in his position to do anything like this so early.

Anastasia Jempelis: It's interesting how much Louise and I agree on these things even though we have not discussed them. I have not used the harmonics as much, but I remember when Dr. Suzuki was telling us about them. He emphasized that a harmonic is a strong tone, not a weak one. We tend to think that it is played lightly with the bow. It can't be played that way because the tone will break.

Louise Behrend: It's very necessary to play firmly with the bow, close to the bridge, to get a strong sound on the harmonics.

Anastasia Jempelis: I teach the scales by rote also, but make a chart of even three-octave scales. The notes are not written down; the fingering only is written down, with the indication to play on the G-string, or D-string, etc. The students find this easy to do.

Louise Behrend: This is a typical example of the way I teach a scale on one string; a stop is made to make the shift, and the fourth finger is stretched to play the last note:

This is a simple way to learn how to move up and down the string very early.

Anastasia Jempelis: I often use the Position Etudes for sight-reading because they are simple to look at.

Louise Behrend: Now let's check whether there are any more questions about introducing the positions. I would like to say something on position technique that is just my own opinion, not Suzuki's. The only reason for not teaching just movement up and down on the instrument without regard to specific positions is sight-reading, where you have to relate fingers across strings. Therefore, I see no reason for not teaching every finger chromatically up the instrument in the final analysis. I think the string bass has a little more sensible arrangement in that every half step is basically a new position. I think the idea of seven positions is a false concept.

Question: When you first shift backwards, does the thumb move first?

Louise Behrend: If you notice, I left that absolutely up in the air. Dr. Suzuki, himself, does not say anything about it. As you all know, there are different schools of shifting. Should the thumb advance? Should the thumb advance only when shifting down? Should it advance going both ways—up and down? There are different opinions on all these points. Successful violinists shift in a variety of ways. Dr. Suzuki seems to keep the hand all in one piece when he shifts. He says, "The less I think about the thumb, the better off I am, as long as it is released." I find that it does help in releasing the thumb to think of it as moving a fraction ahead, especially on the downshift. I do not go as far as many teachers I know who actually do a very complex advance thumb motion. The teachers who use that method are, for the most part, those who feel that there are two points of contact with the violin, the collar bone and the thumb, so that they are going to have to support with an advance movement of the thumb. Ricci and Fuchs are among the violinists who shift this way. On the other hand, Oistrakh and others do not do it that way. There is no fixed rule. The important thing is that the thumb must not be late; it must not be left behind in shifting, and it must be free. The results either way will be good. This point is related to the basic technique of the player and is quite individualistic. I always say "I have no rule of thumb!"

Anastasia Jempelis: One of the supplementary books that is printed in Japan and imported by Summy-Birchard is the *Quint Etudes,* a book with studies based primarily on the intervals of the fourth and the fifth. I usually use this book when the students are in Book V or Book VI. Fifths are difficult to play in tune on the violin owing to the curve of the finger-board as well as to the curve of the finger. For example, if I put my finger down on B-natural and then move it to F-sharp without realizing that I am moving it not in a direct line across, but in a slanted way, I will play it slightly sharp. So I must have the sensation of pulling it back. This must happen each time I play a perfect fifth across the string. This is a physio-psychological thing. Actually, if you measure the distance from the second finger on the B-natural to the second finger on F-sharp on the D-string, it will be directly across, but it seems to the player to be slightly curved in. This is a very important factor in intonation and tremendously important in double stops.

The *Quint Etudes* has exercises dealing with this problem; the exercises go through the seven positions. There are other special problems treated in this book also, for example, the problems of the weak fourth finger and the correct (posturing) positioning of the hand. Special exercises for these problems and others are set down in this book.

Question: Does Dr. Suzuki have the student support the hand against the violin in the third position?

Anastasia Jempelis: It depends on the hand.

Louise Behrend: It also depends on the length of the arm in relation to the violin.

THE VIBRATO

Anastasia Jempelis: As you know, for too long pupils have been told that vibrato is an emotional urge; that it will just come when it is needed. Please don't be optimistic and think that the vibrato is just going to happen magically. In the six years that I have been doing the Suzuki approach at Eastman, I have found that the students have often learned it by observing me use the vibrato. I have often been asked, "Do you vibrate for the children even though they are not vibrating yet?" Of course you do; you are training the ear by doing this. Eventually the student will want to know when he can shake his hand as you do, and eventually he will feel the need of the vibrato, perhaps in the Seitz concertos, if not before. Let him do it if he wants to do it and if his tone is otherwise good.

Before a good vibrato can be cultivated, the hand position and the fingering have to be right. Everything works together to produce a good vibrato: the position of the body, the posture, the way the instrument is held, the left arm and elbow. If there is poor posture or the position of the body is not right, there will be trouble with the vibrato. There should be no distortion of the hand or arm; the hand should not be pulled away from the neck, nor the thumb away from the neck. A good basic hand position and the correct slant of the fingers are essential for a good vibrato. Some students turn the fingers inward too much. This is one reason why it is so beneficial to set the intervals of the fourth and the fifth correctly in the hand. An important factor in cultivating a good vibrato is the first joint of the finger; this should be flexible yet firm. A good exercise to make this joint flexible is to let it move back and forth on chromatic semitones, sliding slowly.

A good vibrato is a combination of arm, hand, and finger action. Your vibrato should have width, the width of the oscillation, plus the intensity or the speed that you use.

The thumb can be a paralyzing factor for the vibrato. If it clutches tightly, or if the hand is tight, the whole left arm and hand are paralyzed.

The left hand moves vertically and horizontally. The vertical movement includes the finger drop which should be firm but not dropped with a hammer-like stroke. If the drop is too hard the joint which should be flexible will be stiff. Horizontal movements include such adjustments as finger extensions and half-steps within one position. String crossing also provides a problem for the vibrato.

It is important to realize that the vibrating movement is from the pitch downward and back up to the pitch; it does not go above the pitch. This is a controversial point but I feel definitely that the vibrato is a backward swing of the left hand.

Louise Behrend: I have very definite reasons for doing the vibrato the way I am going to explain. I have been told that on the East Coast we vibrate up and down, but that on the West Coast they vibrate back and forth on either side of the pitch. Someone has truthfully said, however, that in any case, it is the leadership of the teachers in the area that define this.

I would like to point out three things: (1) We are all agreed that there must be flexibility in the end-joint of the finger. If you move that end-joint forward you are inclined to lock it and push up toward the nail. However, if you pull back you free that joint, (2) We know that the people who have a lush sound are the people who have big pads on their fingers because this is the vibrating part which gives the best tone; and (3) Studies have proved that our ears are inclined to hear the top part of a sound or pitch. If you are vibrating from the top back and going up to the top again, the top pitch is the one you hear because that is the pitch alteration. If you go north of the pitch the sound is a little sharp. This is the psychology of pitch-hearing or discrimination. We tend to hear the soprano before we hear the bass in a composition.

We have different styles in performance just as we have different styles in clothes. Those styles are defined by the existing norms of a given period. Our ears get used to what is in fashion. We wouldn't, for instance, tolerate today the kind of playing that existed before Ysaye, where the player only vibrated on certain notes. The continuous vibrato is as recent as that. Kreisler carried the development of the vibrato one step further by bringing it into passage-work.

Although the continuous vibrato is a recent development, it is a misconception to think that the vibrato is new. If you read Leopold Mozart and his conception of vibrato, you will see that the vibrato has been an important part of the concept of good violin tone for a long time.

Anastasia Jempelis: A book on vibrato from which I extract ideas is *Basic Vibrato Studies* by Louis Stoelzing, published by Belwin-Mills. In this book basic steps to acquiring a good vibrato are set down: (a) silent exercises of waving goodbye; (b) starting in the third position; (c) illustrations of correct and incorrect wrist position; (d) use of the metronome, etc.

Stoelzing's idea is that the vibrato should be continuous and his book is geared to that goal. I don't agree with some of his opinions; for example, with the point he makes in writing out B-sharp, B-flat, etc. ("think sharp, think flat") and in urging the student to think that way. This might tend to bad intonation eventually if such a literal notation is visualized in the student's learning mechanism.

Louise Behrend: With Dr. Suzuki, I'm inclined to feel about this the way I feel about many of the technical exercises written for the violin. We can get the students to practice a very great deal of technique if we do not put an abundance of dull material in front of them. They're perfectly happy to practice technical exercises that are every bit as dull as Sevcik as long as they don't have any of the dull-looking material in front of them. Their interest is rightly in the music, not on the dullest kind of a visual picture which presents itself with many of the standard exercise books.

Question: Would you care to mention any other books that the teachers might get that would be of help?

Louise Behrend: There is a book by Goby Eberhardt *"Violin Vibrato"* (Carl Fischer) which treats of many subjects, not just vibrato. Carl Flesch in his *The Art of Violin Playing,* has much to say on the vibrato that is excellent. Gruenberg also has said a lot about vibrato. The vibrato has been treated in many books written on the violin, but Stoelzing's is the only one specifically on the vibrato that I know of. It is an exercise book to give to the student to work on. Personally, I prefer my own way of giving the students my specific vibrato exercises than to use the book as a workbook.

Anastasia Jempelis: Dr. Suzuki introduces the vibrato in the first position with the third finger on A, then changes to second position at once, then to third position in the following manner:

You start with the third finger, loosening the other two; then put the second finger on the same note, then the first.

Louise Behrend: The question is frequently asked as to when to teach vibrato. I think that you should teach vibrato when the child's hand is positioned well and is strong enough. This can be variable, depending on the physical abilities of the child. There are strong hands and weak hands. With the strong hand you need do very little to strengthen it further; with the weak hand, much often has to be done to build and strengthen it. It depends on the child's physical readiness and not just on emotional readiness as to when you teach the vibrato. Unless the child is physically ready, he may do something wrong such as a forced motion, or a tension reaction, or a gripping hold on the violin. If the position is basically a correct one, the training of the vibrato motion should not be difficult.

It should be remembered that the player vibrates on a diagonal. The movement is not back and forth but diagonal to the string.

Anastasia Jempelis: I mentioned before that the vibrato should be continuous from one note to the other; the hand should be kept moving.

Louise Behrend: I am going to show you some of the procedures which I have found are successful in teaching the vibrato. Don't expect everything to be equally successful with each student. A vibrato does not happen overnight. Dr. Suzuki says that maybe in ten years he will have the answer to vibrato.

The trill which Anastasia mentioned as being a good exercise for the vibrato is indeed helpful. The reason for this is that it helps produce the flexibility needed not only in the end joint of the fingers but in all of the joints. If there is any point of limitation of movement, there will be a limitation of something in the vibrato. The trill therefore, helps the knuckles to be flexible and free and this is necessary for a good vibrato. The rigidly set hand will have difficulty in acquiring a vibrato because the joints are not free. Everything must give.

When I was growing up there was a controversy over which was correct, the arm vibrato or the wrist vibrato. I think there is general agreement today that a good vibrato implies freedom in all of the hinges. This means that there is some arm, some hand, and some finger action involved in the vibrato if you have a viable vibrato, that is, one that will do what you want it to do. Casals says, "You must control your vibrato. It must not control you."

I start preparing the child for the vibrato long before I start teaching the vibrato. Usually a perceptive child will ask very early in his training period when he can "shiver" or "shake." When that happens, I tell him, "As soon as your hands are strong and well-secure on the instrument, we will learn the vibrato. Meanwhile, I am going to get you ready for it." That solves the problem of the student's trying to do it too soon by himself, and you are satisfying him that he is starting to learn the vibrato.

One of the most difficult things to achieve with the student is the loosening of the wrist and fingers. I teach the vibrato first from the wrist and the fingers and then later add the arm motion. My initial exercises may be rhythmic knocking exercises (for example, knock the rhythm of the first variation or any of the variations of "Twinkle, Twinkle Little Star"). Such motions are wider than you would use with the actual vibrato. This is a good, free movement. The thumb is not held against the violin, of course, in this.

There is also the peg-knocking exercise. You hold the violin partly supported by the right hand; lean the thumb hard here in first position so that it is firm and does not move, and go back and simply knock the pegs.

Then there are the gliding exercises. I do them first without fingers on the fingerboard, just moving the arm up and down. Then I place a finger on the string and let it lightly skate up and down. The thumb moves very lightly with the finger.

What I'm doing here is a basic arm motion in the vibrato, even though I teach a wrist and finger vibrato at first. By moving the arm this way I am freeing the wrist and fingers. For some time I have the student do the skating exercises and when he arrives in the higher positions, I have him do hand-waving exercises. Now the thumb is held in one position but there are no fingers down yet.

Then we do what I like to call the "monkey-hanging exercise." You hold the violin like a guitar and let the weight of the arm hang; then let the arm swing. This gives you a combination movement. Even though it is not in the position we are going to use on the violin, it is a freeing exercise, especially for the thumb hinge.

Another helpful exercise is to have someone, or even the student himself, hold the thumb and then wave the hand. This is done with the violin in playing position. Again, this is a helpful exercise in freeing the thumb especially.

Meanwhile, I will have the student playing in the positions so that he has achieved a certain freedom in getting around on the violin. As I mentioned previously, this is done even though his pieces may still be in the first position only.

There comes the day when I find that the student is ready for the vibrato in earnest. The hand is strong; the position is good; he is secure and there is no reason to prevent his starting the vibrato.

The first thing I do is to play a nice tone, using the vibrato, and I ask him if he can imitate what I have played. If he is one of the few who can do this immediately, I ask him to do the same thing on the long notes in the piece he may be playing. When I say that about 2% imitate the vibrato immediately, that is just about the ratio I have met in my teaching experience. You are going to have to teach the vibrato to the other 98% very systematically to have it develop as it should. Most children will achieve something because they want it, but usually it will be faulty because they cannot control it. To the question "What do you consider a faulty vibrato," I answer "A vibrato is faulty if it cannot be controlled." I do not say that it is faulty if more arm is used than I use, or if it is wider basically than my vibrato, but with Casals, I say that a faulty vibrato is one that cannot be controlled.

I start the children with the basic exercise by Rivarde, famous violin teacher of the 19th Century. Flesch quotes this exercise. I find that in most cases it is better to start in the fourth position than in the third. Like Anastasia, I am of the school which teaches the hand movement from pitch to flat position alteration.

Question: How do singers vibrate when they sing? What does the natural voice do?

Behrend: I know what it sounds like, but I don't know what they do because I don't know anything about singing. Does anyone here?

Answer: A proper vibrato in the voice depends on breath control; it is from the diaphragm.

Behrend: I've always thought that the well-produced voice innately has a vibrato. Vibrato is pulsation and there is a pulsation in a beautiful voice.

Other: Vocal authorities say that there are very fine voices that do not have a natural vibrato. The vibrato may be acquired through specific exercises.

Behrend: A basic vibrato, and by that I mean not one that you use to emphasize something special in a tone, but your basic sound, should not be heard as a vibrato. A vibrato should grow out of the natural vibration of the tone. We should not hear an obvious vibrato, either obviously fast or obviously slow. It should just be an enhancing of the natural vibration of the tone. You never heard beautiful vibratos, such as Kreisler's and others, as obvious; the tone became enhanced and enriched in a shimmering sort of way. You want at times more intensity in a vibrato just as you do in a voice for emphasis or excitement. You vibrate differently because you hear it differently.

Comment: I don't think a vibrato is inherent in anything, whether it is the voice or an instrument. It is something cultivated. If you think of the pure singing voice, it is the child's soprano voice; it does not have a vibrato. Also, the basic sound of the wind player is the non-vibrato sound. He is in deep trouble if he doesn't have a straight tone and if he plays with a vibrato only.

Behrend: You have to have a non-vibrated tone. You have to be able to turn off or control the vibrato. Many get into the position of where the vibrato controls them; it can't be stopped at will. In trying to correct my own vibrato the first thing I had to do was to play without any vibrato at all.

To return now to specifics, let me repeat that I start the oscillation on the pitch and roll backwards to the flat position of the tone. I start the initial exercises in the fourth position on the A-string because here the hand lies most comfortably and naturally. On the E-string the hand is likely to feel a little cramped and on the D and G-strings, somewhat stretched.

I tell the student to put the base of the hand against the bottom of the shoulder of the violin so that it is firmly set. The first movement I am going to teach is the combination wrist and finger movement. We start with a very careful placement of the finger, slanted, and explain that the movement will be diagonal. This will mean that the backward movement frees the hand because you are moving diagonally in the direction of the joint, in a way that the hinges will open freely. This will give you maximum flexibility. It also takes care of the problem of "gripping;" you cannot move away freely and grip the violin at the same time.

I usually start with the second finger because it is one of the strongest and therefore the easiest with which to start. I teach at first a very measured oscillation with the stipulation that it must not stop. I use an illustration that always seems to work: if you take a small hard little rubber ball, put it on the table and roll it with a lot of pressure on it, this is the way your finger-tips should feel. The finger has to be firm on the string and you pull back away from it.

This brings me to another preliminary exercise that I have often used with students. It helps to develop the feeling of the pull from the finger-tips and the movement of the hand.

Take both hands, put the wrists together with the left thumb over the right thumb, Let the vibrating finger of the left hand grab the right thumb and snap back and forth. This stretches all the fingers and does not allow any joint to lock. When the finger does the same movement on the string it is active-backward, passive-forward. The sound should be like a whine or a siren; it is not the measured sound of one semitone to another.

Start playing the continuous oscillating movement, using each finger in turn except the fourth. With some students it might be well to practice only with the second finger for a while; if he returns for his next lesson with that well-controlled, give him the first and third fingers.

The length of the fourth finger will determine its vibrato movement. With a very short fourth finger most of the movement comes from the knuckle at the base of the hand and with the finger flat.

When the vibrato movement is beautifully round and controlled and when you don't hear a specific pitch but rather a rolling sound, it may be done on the D-string and the G-string. I leave the E-string until last because of the slightly cramped feeling of the hand that might result when playing on that string in the fourth position. When playing on the G-string the student will have to swing his left elbow quite far in toward the body in order to reach comfortably. This is especially true with smaller children.

These preliminary stages of vibrato-study may take quite a long time. If you take one finger at a time and one string at a time the student has a sense of build-up and continuity in the development of his vibrato. The teacher should not have the student practice such exercises for too long at a stretch. I usually advise that the exercise or routine I'm giving them be practiced at two or three different times in their practice period, for example in the beginning, in the middle, and at the end, so that it is not done too long at a stretch, but more often. Then when the movement is accurate, I start building up the speed. I do this with specific rhythms. I use the metronome with older students but not with the children. I want to be sure that this movement is rhythmic. I want them to feel the rhythmic pulsation, and I start with this type of exercise:

Then I try triplets and sextuplets. This is not yet a vibrato. It is not quite fast enough, but we're building up the activity and the movement.

When a student reaches the point that he has the above speeds secure with all fingers on all strings, then he is ready to move his hand away from the body of the instrument. I usually have the student move directly back to the first position. Occasionally, I have him go back through the third position, then the second, and finally the first.

One means I use to take care of the transition away from holding the hand and arm against the violin in the fourth position is the following: slip the arm between the rungs of a chair until the fore-arm is caught around the middle by the top of the back. This supports the arm so that the hand may vibrate in the same manner as it did when the violin supported it in the fourth position. A bannister, or railing, or anything that will catch the arm and hold it firmly will work as well.

When the student is able to play the above exercises in the three speeds, I set the metronome faster and explain that his first speed is going to be faster than before. I don't move up by the metronome; I move up by the rhythmic series with the faster tempo. That usually results rather quickly in a nice controlled vibrato. That means usually that the student can vibrato on a long note in a piece and sustain it. At the same time he should practice a series of long notes, for example, a scale series, and vibrato in a sustained way on each note.

Question: What do you do when a student comes to you with a reasonably developed arm vibrato?

Behrend: It depends on the quality of the arm vibrato. You say reasonably developed. If it is a beautifully controlled vibrato that he can play any speed and stop when he wants to and all that, I would leave him alone. If I find that it is faulty in any way, and that he cannot control it, I would give him some specific exercises for control. If the student has a good sound and basically, a good movement, why should I change it? As a matter of fact, if a student does not have some arm involvement in his vibrato, I try to bring this about. The vibrato that is only hand, wrist and finger also lacks something.

Question: Do you find that the arm vibrato has a relationship to the hand?

Behrend: I find that it has more relationship to the length of the arm. a friend of mine who plays both the violin and the viola, prefers to teach the arm vibrato from the start. She has an arm vibrato when she plays the violin but when she plays the viola, she has a hand vibrato. The extension made the difference in the way her arm felt. I have noticed that the long-armed, long-handed people tend more often to more arm useage than the short-armed people. I am not stating this as a scientific fact but merely as an observation.

Question: Does not this type of wrist vibrato in forte passages with heavy bowing sometimes become an arm vibrato?

Behrend: Yes, exactly. That is because it is adaptable and the arm is free to move. As a matter of fact, with more intensity, practically everybody will bring more arm into play in the vibrato, and certainly in the upper positions where there is very little play in the wrist, the arm will be more involved.

Question: Is there no way of getting a good arm vibrato unless you have first a good wrist vibrato?

Behrend: I wouldn't say that. I say that it is possible to start with an arm vibrato and still maintain flexibility in the wrist. I happen to have more success in starting with the wrist and fingers. I have seen more people with wrist tension who were started with an arm vibrato than those who were started with the wrist vibrato.

Among others, these two problems emerge in learning the vibrato: the problem of vibrating on a long note after a rapid finger passage and the problem of the continuous vibrato. For the former problem short rapid scale-like passages concluding on a long vibrated note should be part of the daily practice routine. For the problem of the continuous vibrato, long slurred notes should be played with a slow oscillating movement at first and connecting each note with the next in a continuous movement of the hand. The speed should gradually be increased.

There will always be the student who cannot vibrate beyond a certain rate of speed and intensity. Speed build-up for example, with the metronome, somehow does not seem to help. The best thing for this type of student is quick finger exercises, fast trill studies, quick impulse passages and pieces or studies calling for intense fast bowing. Gradually the speed of reaction and the feeling of intensity should begin to develop and this should involve the left arm in quicker action.

The important thing is trying to make practice a regular part of the daily schedule, just as eating meals at certain hours and going to bed at a certain time become part of the child's life style. A family with only one child can accomplish this more easily than the family with several children. Life is better regulated, in a way.

Constance Starr

Chapter 7

Helping Children to Develop Self-Direction in Violin Study

John Kendall

"Ultimately, every violinist is self-taught."

One of the biggest responsibilities of adults, whether teachers or parents, is to understand what is involved in building technique from the musical composition, encouraging the young violinist to grow and mature through *self-directed* practice and study. This concept is basic to our use of the Suzuki method. In the absence of this understanding of self-direction, a teacher may need to use traditional etude material, rather than allow mediocrity, careless and ill-prepared playing.

My early violin study involved the use of three books of Kayser, two Mazas, two Wohlfahrt, five Hohmann, three Gruenberg, and an assortment of Dont, Dancla, Hřimalý and other materials as preparation for Kreutzer. I stacked them in my library after spending hundreds of hours of practice on them. Now in the Suzuki method, we have relieved the young student of this "manufactured" music. But what are we putting in its place to build technique? All too frequently, the teacher supplies nothing, but instead, skips from one piece to another. eliminating some pieces entirely and forgetting that we have a responsibility to build technique, control, and musical understanding through carefully related literature. My plea to parents and teachers is this: make each piece into an interesting and rewarding *study,* as well as a musical experience.

The beginning approach to the child for both parents and teachers, should be guided by the policy: *"Ask* the child, don't *tell* him."* This is not an escape from discipline, but a use of creative discovery as an alternative to the barren "You must do this" approach. Under such an externally structured regimen the child will accomplish many things, and if he is tractable he will follow directions, but even if he seems to have reached the goal there is an essential shortcoming. He will have missed the discovery of certain qualities within himself.

The central problem is this: how can we, as teachers, respect the immeasurable potential inherent in human beings from the first day of their lives? Conversely, how can we avoid that destructive manner which so often passes for teaching but which is, in effect, ruthless domination of one spirit by another? The simplest pieces in the Suzuki method, or in any other method for that matter, give us our opportunity to discover in each piece the essential new point and not to bypass it. A teacher who thinks that a piece has no particular purpose or "teaching point" probably hasn't understood it, and needs to re-examine it. If the teacher passes over the "Children's Song" for example, without teaching the idea that there is a beautiful phrase group connected by "hooked" or "linked" bowing, then the child will be surprised later on by the problem of hooked bowing in "The Happy Farmer," and he will accomplish it with great difficulty. To assist the child with this basic bowing when it is *first* encountered, it should be taken out of context and repeated many times until it is completely integrated into his playing.

Another example of "unpreparedness" is often revealed in the "national disaster area" of the D sharp measure of "Judas Maccabeus." Often the students have not fully appreciated the "close 3-4" finger pattern that they learned when playing the Bach "Minuets," so they are not ready to build on it in the later pieces. To help them, go back to the "Minuets" and say, "How did you do that?" (referring to the close 3-4 pattern). They explain, review the pattern again, and soon are ready for progress with the new piece.

Implicit in all of these examples is the skilled and imaginative process of taking an idea and building it into exercise material. If you truly want to accomplish this building process, my suggestion would be to first of all separate the right from the left hand. Which one is the problem? The child really doesn't always know. In fact, even a college student may not know.

How can the student be helped to become an active partner in his own teaching process? Fundamentally, through the questions that the teacher asks, such as: "How can you do this?" Ultimately, every violinist is self-taught. No teacher can give final answers; he can only help the student along the arduous road of self-discovery.

Students begin to solve their own problems at the age of five or six. A child does not have to be a genius to answer the question: "Why do we lift and set the bow?" Almost all will think of reasons: "To keep the shoulder relaxed. To keep the bow balanced. To watch how far from the bridge. To come in for a landing gently. To make a good tone." This is more useful in every way than telling the child, "You must lift and set."

If at a lesson the teacher says to the student, "Practice this fifteen times," the parent has two options upon returning home: "Practice 15 times the way the teacher told you." or, "What was it the teacher told you to practice?" The latter, of course, is preferable. If in response to it the child says vaguely, "Something about my finger," perhaps he has forgotten. The parent's reply need not impose information upon him. Rather, the child could be questioned: "Was it on the E string? Was it with the first finger?"

Keep "priming the pump " (it may take a cupful, or gallons!). He will say, at last, "That was it—the first and third fingers." But don't stop. Say "Why did the teacher have you practice that?" He may answer, "To get my third finger in the right place." With that statement he has become involved in a process. The parent has succeeded.

It is surprising how much teaching is made possible through

questions. Because of them, the student will begin to explore, to improve; and at that point, when he is given new information, the teacher is not force-feeding him, but dining together at the same table. Children enthusiastically accept this equality.

Discussing the *character* of the music is another area for student involvement. "What character?", he may say, "it doesn't describe anything." Help him again with choices: "Is it weak and quiet, or strong and loud?"

He can find out, and he needs to understand the inner character of the music to perform it well. Again, "discovery" techniques are useful. The teacher may use alternatives playing a passage in two different styles and asking: "Which way do you like the music to sound?" How much better this is than bluntly saying "Do it this way." The teacher who works primarily through directives and imperatives may be stultifying, not liberating the child's imagination and musicality.

Alternatives are better than absolutes. Make it clear to the child *why* we are practicing a certain way and *what* is being solved. It isn't the letter, but the spirit of the law that we seek.

In relation to this, I hear so many teachers and parents searching for the absolute answers. "Where can we find the "pure Suzuki?", they ask. It seems to me the proper answer is "Nowhere." Of course, there are basic principles, and established repertory, but like any other growing, changing concept, the Suzuki method does not exist exclusively as a measurable, definable entity. It is a spirit. Its position today may be different from the one of yesterday. It lives in its philosophy, not in its substance. To illustrate, we might recall the professor who gave a lecture directly contradicting one of his books. A courageous student raised his hand and pointed this out. "Young man," the professor answered, "I wrote that book five years ago, and five years is a long time in the life of a thinking man."

In the case of Dr. Suzuki, five years *is* a long time, and he *is* a thinking man. He is a growing, changing, evolving teacher, like any other good teacher. Watching his work over a period of years one notices many developments, some changes, some adjustments, and always new fresh ideas. No teacher who is looking for a neat, complete pure "Suzuki package" will ever find it. If, however, he is looking for the spirit of the teacher— how to reach the child, how to make him involved, to give him happiness, to help him solve his problems, to analyse his needs —then he may find something extremely important.

Thus, a skilled teacher shows a child how to play the Suzuki "Allegro," based on the child's needs at the moment, while the recording gives a somewhat different interpretation. Which is "correct"? Both may be, since each performance aims at its own level of learning. Understanding the different "levels of musical sophistication" through which an oft-reviewed composition may be studied takes considerable imagination, and thought on the part of the teacher. Many teachers would prefer to be "programmed" rather than to be inventive.

Parents, too, fall into the "pure package" misconception. Sometimes they say to me, "When will our child get out of the Suzuki method?" The implication is that the method is a kind of pedagogical box into which we put the child, and from which, after shaking and baking him about for a few years, we allow him to emerge, all crispy and crunchy, for the next phase of his development.

Parents and teachers who share this concept think of Suzuki as something that is "complete" at some point. They have failed to see that this is a *way of learning,* an approach to the instrument and to the child. The spirit of study and performance, unlike the precise moment when the student finished Volume 10, will last a lifetime. He will build on it in a thousand unforeseen ways.

Dr. Suzuki has said that when his advanced students go to study with another teacher they should be ready to grow. This is a sensible attitude, much different from the repressive one often found among teachers who tend to be jealous of their work. Such teachers don't want the student to go to another teacher—they want him to be a "possession." Of course, that is not the way spirited teachers should think of a child, whether in the larger relationship, or in regard to lessons.

A child is less apt to "find out" for himself than a college student. He must be helped to make decisions himself. It may be the bow hand. If so, the first step is to reduce the problem to open strings. What is the stroke? If the child is playing "May Song" this is the first time he has used a dotted quarter and eighth. We might tell the students that the eighth note is a "lightning stroke." With bow pointed toward the ceiling, make the stroke in the air together until they get the feeling of the dotted rhythm. The right arm is the best metronome available, if we build the rhythms into it. So the basic problem is isolated and solved in its simplest form.

Next, the problem occurs on two strings. Measure that crossing. Get the student's arm loose. Then after doing this many times, put the second finger on the A string. The child then has a whole series of things to practice in order to get the basic point of this piece. If it is a bow problem, reduce it to open strings. If it is a left-hand problem, eliminate the slurs or other intricate bowings. Use the motto "one bow per note." If there is trouble, reduce everything to that level, without rhythm. Then the child thinks of finger patterns and how the fingers work together in units, rather than as separate and confusing entities.

To summarize: First, separate the problems. Next, reduce bow problems to the open strings, and get the basic stroke. If the problem is in the left hand, reduce it to one bow per note. Finally, combine bow and left hand.

We often tell the students, "Practice slowly," but that is only one of about a dozen ways to practice well. If we constantly fall back on "slowly" our teaching is bankrupt. Often *fast* practice is better!

I once saw Dr. Suzuki teach a student who was playing "Perpetual Motion" by pushing the tempo faster and faster, crowding, until this little child, to his own great surprise and pleasure, managed to perform the piece he could not play slowly!

For a child beginning violin study in the traditional way, life is a perpetual adagio. Why? He wants to *move*, but this leads to practicing too fast. If he is making mistakes, he should think in units. Fast practice implies units. The mind boggles at great surges of notes, but not if the notes are divided into sensible units. The good teacher can tell what the unit is. It may be rhythmic groupings, phrase groupings, all notes on one string, or between shifts in position, or in one finger pattern, etc. The child should practice rhythmically, yet with sufficient space between units to enable him to think about his problem. When helping a child with unit practice, don't stop the repetition process to lecture: "Your bow isn't right. Your left hand isn't right. Your feet aren't right." It is better to establish a pace, and then during the rests between units, interject ideas or corrections. This will help him towards self-direction in his practicing.

Changing the bowing is very important. Putting in holds, accents, and rhythms are ways that the teacher can help the child in the simpler pieces. All good teachers must become masters of this technique, particularly if they are going to teach under the Suzuki method. One goal is to dramatize the problem, to make it real to the child, and to get him involved in practicing. If a teacher is insecure about one of the Suzuki compositions and cannot do this, he may find it necessary to use some etude materials. There is no reason why such materials should not supplement the Suzuki books. If a child is ten or twelve years old, and is advanced in the Suzuki method, he will probably be in a junior high orchestra in about a year. We have a real responsibility to help that student broaden his sense of musical styles, and his reading skills.

The Doflein Books have been helpful in this respect. This series is organized as follows: Book I—very easy exercises and duets; Book II—slightly more difficult; Book III—2nd and 3rd positions; Book IV—more advanced techniques; Book V—higher positions. Unlike etude materials that contain primarily all 19th century German and French pedagogy, and provide only

By comparing violin playing to archery, John Kendall vividly demonstrates for students the proper angle of instruments to their bodies.

one basic style, the Doflein books use music from Monteverdi to Bartok, from Palestrina to Carl Orff and other contemporaries. The student learns many different musical styles, how to play in 5/8 and 7/8 and other rhythms, and various modes. There are also many duets so that the teachers can play with the student.

I don't think that the use of such books is removed from the spirit of Dr. Suzuki's teaching, for it is supplementary and harmonious with the main trend of the materials. Many American teachers offer two basic criticisms of the Suzuki materials: (1) All of the early materials are in the easy keys; (which make the violin "sound," and are the free, open keys), but if the student is going into an orchestra, he will need experience with the other keys; (2) they do not include much contemporary music. There may be a simple answer to the latter complaint—the matter of copyright. I think we should not hesitate to look for contemporary material to use in an intelligent way at the right level.

How important is tonalization? The essence of violin playing is tone, and when we practice any bow exercises, we are undertaking tonalization. This process, in my opinion, should not be separated from the composition being studied, but should grow out of it. I urge teachers to help the student to tonalize, not only in isolation, but in order to make a specific piece sound better. Tonalization exercises can be built out of each piece. Then they become real. Unable to think of anything else to say about a player, a New York newspaper critic recently ended his article with: "He had a small but scratchy tone." That is the antithesis of what we want with Suzuki students. Suzuki wants the tone to be the central idea, not a peripheral one.

How many repetitions does a child have to make in his home practice? How can the student be encouraged to practice tonalization? We often say to him, "Let's do this a lot," but we don't really dramatize it for him. Dr. Suzuki's charming way is to tell the student, "We will do this ten practice times, counting: "one, two, two and a half, three," etc. The child gets the idea very quickly. Ten "practice times" means many, many more than ten. The child himself can supply an answer that will itself help to motivate him, when the question is raised: "How do you know when you have practiced enough?" Then he has to decide when the music sounds right, when it begins to feel comfortable. Most students do not repeat enough, nor do teachers ask them to do so because we are so hurried at the lessons. We don't want to take lesson time to repeat things that "he'll do at home." But it is necessary to repeat *at the lesson,* and the parent must be helped to understand that repetition is needed both at the lesson and at home.

How long should the children practice? Americans, rushing everywhere, taking little time to enjoy their pleasures, often pass on their time concept to their children. As their prosperity increases, even the Japanese are taking less time to enjoy deeply.

What is time? To the youngster, it is relative. You say, "Did you practice this week? How long? Show me." The student plays the phrase twice. "Do you think that if you practiced that phrase for thirty seconds that would be too much?" you ask. Putting the watch on him, he will find that thirty seconds allows a good deal of repetition! But he is willing to practice that long because he knows it is really a short time. When he repeats something he has to think how to do it better each time. Let him use a clock. Ask, "Do you think you could do that for two minutes?" When he really does it for two minutes he is giving himself a chance. Repetition is so necessary to develop security, skill, understanding, and automatic response.

In American life, perfectionism is rampant. We are all perfectionists about our students. But often we don't accompany that attitude with two other "p's", which are patience and persistence, without which perfectionism is damaging if not actually ruinous. Students and parents are all out for quick success. Children fear the loss of parental approval if they are unable to succeed quickly. They begin to feel inadequate and fall by the wayside. We must train them to have the patience and persistence to do something over and over and to feel that this is natural. Even a genius has to repeat.

We can really help the students by giving them a step-by-step feeling of accomplishment. Above all, students must not be made to feel that the teacher's or the parent's love and affection are contingent upon success. This is often implied by over-eager teachers and parents who are anxious for students to succeed. The child begins to feel that he must succeed or his parents won't care for him. Many of the more sensitive students won't take the risk and therefore won't even try. Few parents realize that their very urging often frightens the student away from attempting something. As parents, we all walk the tightrope of how to encourage and help the children without making them feel that we love them only if they are successful.

When the teacher has an unthreatened, open spirit, students will sense it. If he gets them involved and permits them as much self-direction as possible. they will respond. In Japan, where children are brought up to have tremendous respect for the word of the teacher and not to ask "Why?" the Japanese teacher may not be able to use some of the devices we have been discussing. But in America our children are not brought up this way. They don't have an ingrained conviction that everything the teacher says is right—no questions asked. It is important for us to take advantage of the spirit of inquiry among our students, using it to say, "You look for the answers," getting them involved, helping them teach themselves. In this way, our teaching can be more enjoyable and productive.

A teacher must be able to answer "why" when he is asked. If he can't, he probably hasn't thought through the problem in terms of his own playing and teaching. That doesn't mean he always has to answer at the moment the question is asked. He may say, "Well, you do it first and try and we'll talk about it later." But he does not put off the child with a remark that damages the teaching relationship, such as "Don't ask me why, just do it." Teaching should always be in terms of self-discovery.

We must measure every child according to his own ability, rather than in contrast to others. It would be a mistake for us to stop at a certain level with a child who could accomplish much more. It is for us to help that child to reach his true goal. But on the other hand, we must not force another child to go beyond his goal.

Phyllis Glass

In preparation for holding her violin correctly, this beginner places her hand on her right shoulder, right arm at side, while turning her head.

The student places the violin between her chin and shoulder. Her ability to grasp and hold it at the proper angle improves rapidly with practice.

If it is the right size, the instrument will fit snugly in the palm of the left hand when the arm is extended to form a cup for the scroll.

The left hand is
shown here in position,
ready to play.

A teacher shows a student how to place her fingers on the bow. Young students often need much physical assistance as they develop ability.

Beginners place their thumbs outside of the frog, opposite the 2nd and 3rd fingers, diagonal to the stock. The index finger touches the stick between the 1st and 2nd joints. The little finger is above the "dot."

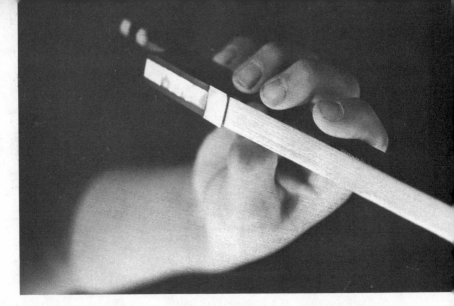

When facility has increased, the student places the thumb under the hair, against the bump of the frog. The thumb nail, but not the pad of the thumb, shows from the front. The thumb is curved but not stiff.

Standing on one foot while playing, is a "game" designed to improve balance and posture.

The placement of the feet that Dr. Suzuki recommends enables the students to achieve comfortable positions that offer good support.

After playing, students return to rest position.

A student places her hand in the First Position and is ready to start the shift to the higher positions.

In the Second Position the fingers are slightly above their place in the First. The first finger is over the C on the A string. The elbow is toward the front of the body. The wrist follows curve of arm.

By the Fourth Position the hand is closer to the violin shoulder, and the first finger is on the E of the A string. The hand touches the shoulder of the violin lightly; the thumb is at the curve of fingerboard.

In the Fifth Position the left elbow is closer to the body, and the wrist is curved up and over the shoulder of the violin. Meanwhile, the first finger is approximately over the edge of the body.

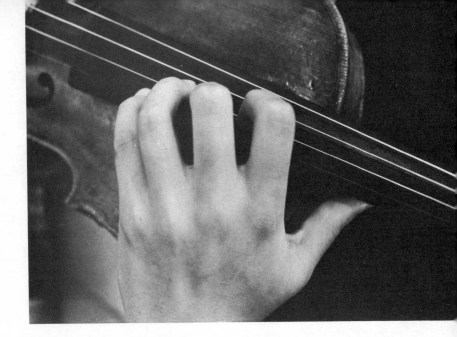

In the Seventh Position the first finger is one octave higher than the open string note. The tip of the thumb is at the front side of the violin neck's curvature. The elbow raises the hand over violin shoulder.

Dr. Suzuki's basis of tone production is the vertical line, or the nearly vertical line, which the violinist can attain only on the E string. The reason was fairly unorthodox in the teaching of beginning violin. It was done to give much more feeling of gravity on the strings. Dr. Suzuki is trying to teach at the very beginning of instruction that bowing is not horizontal. Preparatory exercises and bow games are done with very young children and always in the vertical line. There is now, for example, a "helicopter exercise" in which the child lifts the bow and makes vertical contact with each string. The student's first problem is to point the elbow down as the hand goes way up.

Diana Tillson

Chapter 8

No Child Is Lost

American Suzuki Institute—West

"We know now that every child learns, but not at the same rate. That is, we must give the stimulus that will enable him to learn at his own rate."

In his book, "Nurtured by Love," Dr. Suzuki tells about the parakeet of a Talent Education teacher, Mr. Miyazawa. He wanted to teach it to speak its name, Peeko. After two months and 3,000 repetitions the bird did learn to speak the name. Then Mr. Miyazawa wanted to know whether this first success would lead to others, and he went on to teach the bird its last name, Miyazawa. This is a much harder word, but it took only 200 repetitions. Then the bird learned to cough as its master did.

Suppose the bird's owner had said, "I will try 500 times to teach this bird, and if it fails to speak its name I will take it back to the shop." Peeko would never have learned anything. Too often this is what happens in the education of children. We cross people off. We do not allow for the fact that the absorption rate differs in each person. That is the ultimate importance of Dr. Suzuki's remark, "The only superior ability that a child might have at birth is the speed and sensitivity with which he absorbs his environment."

Dr. Suzuki tells another story about a handicapped girl whose parents wanted to give her musical training. Whenever she reached a certain place in her bowing her hand refused to hold the bow, and she dropped it. Her mother worked terribly hard with the child, but the bow was still dropped. At length

She came to Dr. Suzuki, saying, "What in the world can I do?"
"Pick it up," Dr. Suzuki said calmly.

The mother took the advice. She kept working with the girl, who at length learned to hold the bow well. The story illustrates Dr. Suzuki's philosophy: every child, even a handicapped one, can learn if the stimulus is repeated often enough.

People ask Dr. Suzuki, "Do you test children for musical aptitude before they are accepted?" His answer always is, "No, that would be wrong. Students who at first do not seem to have an aptitude will surprise us later with how well they can do." Every teacher has had students who tempted them to say, "Music just doesn't seem to be the right thing for you." But this continuing feeling that everyone can learn will give a teacher energy to proceed. In the end, observers are always amazed at the accomplishments of these students.

One girl was very stiff and didn't seem to improve at all when playing the violin. Now in her seventh year, she is one of the top students. In the same way, Dr. Suzuki has said that some of the best soloists in his touring groups have been slow starters. One girl spent two years on "Twinkle" alone. That seems like a long time, but afterward she was a fine violinist.

Dr. Suzuki says that *patience,* as we know it, is not the attitude needed to teach the violin, or any other instrument, for that matter. The word implies controlled frustration. We never say, "I am patiently eating a steak." The learning process should be one of enjoyment for teachers and parents, as well as students. It is difficult for us to achieve this. It may be easier for the Japanese because they tend to accept things as they are. We Americans are impatient to see *results;* we want them *now.* If we talk about patience it means that we "sit through it" and try to control our tempers. But as Dr. Suzuki says, the teacher and parent should enjoy each step along the way, especially with a very young child.

Teaching a small child can be a very slow process, and the results are often not known for a long time. But you should, if you can, learn to recognize each small step. You will become excited by each of them. Remember how parents grow excited when their child begins to walk and to talk? "He said his first word today." "He took his first step." This is the way we should regard musical progress.

When a child learns to walk and talk he may be in the only time of life when he is allowed to do things at his own speed. At other times the rate is imposed by adults. In music we often say, "That's enough of this lesson, go on to the next." But we never say to a child, "Now you have said 'mama' fifty times. That's enough, go on to the next word."

It's true that parents become impatient when comparing their child's development with that of others. They may say, "That child walked at nine months and mine didn't until 11 months," but they can't do very much about it. They may lift a child to his feet, but if he is not ready to walk he is going to sit down. He knows from his own inner mechanism that he is not ready, and he will let you know when he is ready. The same is true of talking. Some children may not say a thing for a long time, and their parents become very anxious. Then suddenly the child starts talking and never stops. He has been absorbing words which finally come out.

"We as educators must learn to wait," Dr. Suzuki says. "We are too impatient for results. We should say, 'I will keep giving this child what I think he needs to learn, but I will wait until he is ready.'"

Patience in the common sense should have no part of this at all. We should, instead, have interested, pleasant observations to make.

Dr. Suzuki's discovery that anyone can learn with proper help came early in his career. He had returned from his studies in Germany and was a successful teacher in Japan. One day a father came to him seeking musical education for his four-year-old son, who seemed talented.

Dr. Suzuki asked for time to consider the problem. If this boy can learn Japanese at four, he thought, why not music? Those of you familiar with the Montessori system know that there are "sensitive periods" in children's lives when they are more receptive to certain kinds of learning. We know that very young children are able to learn not only language, but dialect. At that age, then, children must be very sensitive to sound. The four-year-old who was taught by Dr. Suzuki proved him right. This boy became the fine concert violinist, Toshio Eto, who has performed in many parts of the world.

We know now that every child learns, but not at the same rate. That is, we must give the stimulus that will enable him to learn at his own rate. We must know how much stimulus to give each child. When one child needs more stimulus than another we all too often say, "The first is smart and the second is dumb." The second is given no real chance to succeed. Yet in time he probably will succeed, and the results will be amazing.

The Talent Education Institute in Matsumoto, about 150 miles from Tokyo, is a very cosmopolitan area because of the many people who have come to observe music education there. Some psychologists who came to test children at the experimental kindergarten were startled to find that the average IQ of the children was 150! They were sure the scores were wrong and repeated the tests, but the results were exactly the same.

There is now an Early Development pre-school association in Japan, supported by Sony and other companies. It is interested not only in music but in the whole area of early education. This is one reason why the Suzuki method has "caught on." It is not just a way to teach one skill but to give hope and ability and compassion in many areas of life.

The Suzuki method can bring richness and fullness to millions. "I am not trying to train professionals, but to give happiness to all children," Dr. Suzuki has said.

In the past making music "fun" meant setting lower standards. In the Suzuki approach, while the children do have fun, it is not at the expense of excellence. They learn to play well and become very sensitive musicians. They enjoy their study. If they do not become professional musicians, they will nonetheless have had a wonderful experience and probably will enjoy music the rest of their lives.

"We used to dread recitals when we were students," many mothers have said, "Now we really look forward to them."

If children learn to play well, they will enjoy it. We enjoy anything that we do really well.

Children have an inborn eagerness for learning, but we do many things to squelch it by our negativeness. They will strive, and strive indefinitely, to obtain some good effect. This is one of the principal points of Dr. Suzuki's philosophy—it is related to achieving excellence.

Children have the patience; parents often do not. One mother used to ask me whether I had taught a good lesson after each one was completed. I didn't appreciate the question at all. Why was it asked? Didn't she believe in me? Too often we are page-flippers rather than seekers after excellence. "Good," in the minds of many American mothers, means completing a piece or a book, not what it should mean: doing something well.

Margery Aber

Chapter 9

Suzuki Piano Technique

Harlow Mills

". . . early reliance on the memory is very important for developing a sense of security in playing in public."

The Suzuki approach to piano study begins with listening and the development of the ear and the memory. The first pieces are usually learned by rote, giving the student freedom to put all of his attention on tone, shading, and on the technique needed to achieve them. Reading comes a little later, after good playing habits have been established.

One of the most noticeable characteristics of the Suzuki piano students is the fullness and expressiveness of their tone. In a large auditorium their sound fills the hall in the same way that an adult artist's does.

The first exercises and pieces are aimed at tone production. In the first piece, "Twinkle, Twinkle, Little Star" and its variations, the first variation uses a free arm stroke for repeated notes. To gain good quality of tone the arm must be loose, the fingers firm, but the wrist flexible so that the shock of the full-arm motion can be cushioned. The rhythm is four 16ths followed by two 8ths. As this is speeded up the 16ths are played by the forearm moving from the elbow, and the two 8ths are forearm staccato with a high bounce off the key at the end. This rhythm is repeated with each finger until it is well-established. Then it is applied to the notes of "Twinkle, Twinkle," repeating the rhythm, four 16ths and two 8ths on each tone of the melody.

Another motion frequently used is a long drop onto a note with an immediate rebound, giving a very crisp staccato. This is practiced on single notes and also on scales, using the regular scale fingering. If the students miss a note they immediately go back to the beginning of the scale and start over. Therefore, there is a great incentive to gain accuracy. Not only do they learn good aim, but they develop strong fingers and learn to gauge the exact point when they reach the key bed and turn around. From this they develop great freedom of arm motions.

The fingers also are used very actively in scales and passage work. Runs are practiced with quick finger motions and a moment's pause before going on to the next finger for complete preparation. They are also practiced in finger groups, with quick articulation of each note within a small group. Arpeggios, scales, and irregular runs are broken up into small practice units which are played at one impulse.

Great attention is paid to good position of the wrist. It should not be too high, which would make shallow playing, nor too low, which causes the fingers to stick in the bottom of the keys. Generally with young students the problem is too low a wrist. This can be corrected by holding a hand under the child's wrist about a quarter of an inch below the ideal position. Then if the child's wrist starts to drop it will touch the teacher's or parent's hand and be a reminder to get back into position. Do not keep the hand underneath too close, or the student will develop a stiff wrist from not being able to move at all. This would cause jerky, thumpy playing.

It is very important, if the student is to maintain the correct hand position naturally, to have a high enough stool or chair. There should also be a footstool for young students to help them maintain a good sitting posture. If there is not any support for the feet students begin to slump involuntarily and tire more quickly.

Pieces should not be just learned (memorized) and then dropped. They should be kept up, and the teachers should point out ways in which the playing may be improved—better tone quality, more sensitive shading, attention to phrasing, clear dynamic contrasts. They may be played in different octaves on the piano for variety and may also be transposed to other keys. Also, teacher or parent may play one hand while the student plays the other. Or two people may take turns, alternating phrase-by-phrase. There are many ways in which repetition can be varied while still accomplishing the goal of gaining more and more security.

One idea for encouraging repetition is to set up a graduation goal, perhaps at the end of the first book. In order to graduate at that point into the second book the student should be able to demonstrate his ability to play all the pieces in the first book. This can be made a game if other students are present by having them call for different pieces in a random manner for the graduating student to perform. After passing such a test of memory the student will feel a great satisfaction in going on to the next book.

Questions Often Asked About Suzuki Piano

Q. When do you depart from the excessively high motions?

A. As soon as the student has learned the motion well. Then it is incorporated into his technique and used in a way that seems appropriate to the music. Certainly by the second book the motions are not as extreme. But I think it is generally true that the Japanese students play with a great deal of expressiveness and use more technical devices as an aid to this than is common with our American students. As a result, their playing is very interesting to listen to in concert. One can enjoy a children's concert for its musical values.

Q. Is this method as successful with adults as with children?

A. The habits of adults are more established, and it is harder for them to change than it is for children. Adults are also more self-conscious and not likely to feel as much at home with the children's songs in the

Harlow Mills introduces the keyboard to a child who is enrolling in the piano program, a recent development in the Suzuki method.

first volume. By the second volume, however, the music is of a level to appeal to any age. I have had some adults who began because they wanted to help their children and kept on because it was satisfying to them personally.

Q. Are there any special Suzuki approaches to phrasing?

A. There is great attention to nuance, accent, shaded phrase endings and other artistic considerations. The teacher demonstrates musical phrasing and the pupil imitates. Also, the teacher frequently plays along with the pupil so that the sound of nuance is in the pupil's ears *as he plays,* and becomes a part of his concept of the music.

As for phrasing in the sense of deciding when phrases end, and the phrase structure of the music, I did not happen to see this presented to the students when I was in Japan. In teaching a school age student I like to help him discover the structure of a piece, which phrases are repeated, either exactly or with different endings; where the contrasting phrases come; what are the natural "breathing places" of the music and what dynamic contrasts can help to set off the phrase structure. It is best to discover these things first by listening, then by locating them on the printed page and finally by playing. This kind of analysis, even in simple terms the child can understand, is a great help in memorizing, as well as in playing with musical understanding.

Q. To me phrasing means lifting the hand, but I've noticed that Suzuki trained children often go on without a lift.

A. This is sometimes a matter of taste. Sometimes a long note is sufficient indication at the end of a phrase, or a change of dynamics might give the sufficient indication of the end of a phrase. Generally a lift of the hand is the clearest indication of the end of a phrase. A rest certainly should be observed. I tell the students, "A 'rest' means work —the work of picking up your hand."

Q. Suzuki uses many repetitions. Do the students keep practicing everything from the beginning· as they move into the advanced books?

A. No, it isn't possible. In my opinion it is a good idea to practice the whole first book through the end. As you go on always keep some things in review, but not the whole repertoire. The student will always have a fine repertoire from memory. Of course, it is up to the teacher, and the parent, to see that the pieces really improve and don't become carelessly or thoughtlessly played. Even familiar pieces can be used to bring out new qualities. As some new skill is learned on a new piece it might be applied to an old one that has similar elements of interpretation.

Q. What is the first approach to scales?

A. The first approach comes at the beginning of the second book with the C Major scale in the standard fingering. There is no particular instruction there as to how it is taught, except for the rhythm, which stops for a half-note on the keynote; that is a good way of giving the student time to think ahead of fingering patterns. At lessons the children play the scale with a metronome in different speeds, loud and soft, legato and staccato, especially the high, jumping staccato mentioned earlier. One useful approach to scales is to take the three-finger group of notes and play it in all octaves all over the keyboard; then to do the same with the four-finger group. When the two are put together the student is still conscious of the finger grouping.

Q. How are the more advanced books taught by ear?

A. A very common misconception of the Suzuki method is that all learning is done by rote imitation. The students do learn to read, usually by the second book, unless they are very young. The more advanced pieces are learned from notation, with the additional help of listening often to the records of course. Memorizing is expected from the first time that a pupil brings a piece for a lesson. Usually the printed music is not placed on the piano, but is in the mother's hands where she notes down any comments by the teacher. Sometimes it is placed on the piano to call the student's attention to details that have been overlooked. But the playing itself is from memory. This early reliance on the memory is very important for developing a sense of security in playing in public. I have noticed children playing with the greatest composure while being photographed, with flash bulbs popping off constantly. Also, I have observed that they are quite unperturbed by mistakes, but pick themselves up and go right on without a break. Of course, they try very hard not to make mistakes, but if they should make one, it does not cause a disastrous break in the flow of the music.

Q. It is true that the teacher spends no lesson time teaching notes?

A. A great deal is expected of the parents in basic note teaching. However, a teacher may check a child on note recognition. When the parents are responsible for reading, the student is able to gain much more from the lessons; there is more time to give attention to interpretation and technique, Dr. Suzuki says that if the children can play they learn to read more easily. This corresponds to a child's learning to read words whose meaning he already knows. Later he goes on to sound out the unfamiliar words. If he already has a musical vocabulary of melodies, note patterns, chords before he starts to read, then the earliest reading can be a matter of recognition of the symbols for these familiar elements.

Applying the Suzuki concept to the piano, Constance Starr gains exceptional concentration from beginners at the American Suzuki Institute.

Chapter 10

The Use of Recordings and Tape Recordings in Suzuki Training

American Suzuki Institute—West

"Problems in a child's playing are often traceable to the failure to listen enough."

Many children today come from homes where the only music played is rock-and-roll, the background for television shows, or the popular tunes. For them, classical music is an entirely new language. If they are going to understand and play it they must hear it over and over again, until it has become part of their unconscious. Records and tape recordings are essential for all students in the Suzuki method. They are doubly important for children who are being introduced to classical music for the first time.

Dr. Suzuki says that listening is one of the most important elements of musical training. He emphasizes that it should be started at birth. One composition with clear patterns, probably from the Baroque period, can be selected and played often for a baby. If it is, he probably will memorize the piece and make it, and music, too, a part of his life.

After long and careful listening, almost any child can be taught to discriminate between good and bad playing. One boy, when a year old, once said, "That's bad!" when he heard the "Star Spangled Banner" played incorrectly as a joke. Dr. Suzuki, who witnessed the incident, often repeated the story as an example of how quickly children can learn to recognize both good and bad musical qualities.

Japanese children are given tape recordings of Book I, so

that they know the pieces in it by the time they begin the Suzuki program. They have some familiarity with each piece, and less time is needed, as a result, to teach them how to play. More time can be spent on the achievement of fine tone and shading.

A child's listening should be informal. If he is made to sit down and listen for an hour a day he will hate to listen because it is not a pleasant experience. Music should be absorbed casually. Play the Suzuki record during meals or at bedtime. Children who are doing other things may seem not to be listening to the record, but they probably are absorbing it unconsciously.

Problems in a child's playing are often traceable to the failure to listen enough. Recently one of my students had rhythmical trouble, and I expressed surprise, "But, if he is listening to the tape recording," I said, "he should not have had this difficulty." The mother seemed embarrassed. The tape recorder had been broken and he hadn't been listening for the past two weeks, she confessed. As soon as it was fixed he went ahead rapidly with good rhythmic sense.

I ask children with musical problems to listen to their tape or record, then to play and to repeat the process until they have come as close as possible to copying the model. Even when they go on vacation, children can be kept in touch with their studies through the recordings. Sometimes they come back playing better and more musically than when they left. Their listening developed a good tonal sense, but only if the machine had good tone. The better the quality of the model, the better the student's imitation of it.

Portable tape recorders have also proved extremely useful as guides for parents. Taken to lessons, the recorder enables a parent to preserve the way in which the teacher played the piece. Phrasing, tone, and technique become instantly clear. This is especially helpful for parents who do not play.

Listening can be a source of motivation, as well as of correction. Children hear a piece they like, and this makes them eager to study it. Yet, for all of its importance in the Suzuki method, the modern phonograph record or tape has caused some people to wonder whether creativity isn't being stifled by the process of imitation. "Shouldn't older students do more independent thinking?"

Older students will become more creative in the normal process of studying and growing. They will often spend much time and money going to artist teachers because they want to learn about interpretation. Some of the problem of gaining uniqueness is solved easily merely by listening to a variety of recordings. After much listening and analyzing and synthesizing, I create my own interpretations. This is a normal outgrowth of listening.

Interpretation must be learned, just as any other skill is learned. People sometimes say, "Just express yourself;" but if I were handed a strange instrument I would be unable to do so. Although I might feel musically creative I wouldn't know what to do with the instrument. Just as technical skill must be learned in order to play, interpretive skill must be gained before there is self-expression.

It has never seemed to me that listening would stunt musical growth. I see it positively; the children are constantly being given the stimulus of beautiful sounds and phrasing. This process should be continued for a long time. If you have heard Suzuki students and have been impressed by their tone and interpretation, their experience with listening to fine models may be credited. People often ask, "But do they feel the music?" The answer, I think, is "Yes." You can tell that they feel the shape of a phrase by their body movements. These are not affected. They genuinely feel the height of a phrase and the falling away of a cadence. Their movement may seem slightly exaggerated; but this will tone down later.

When I showed one teacher a tape of small children playing beautifully she said, "But do they know how to read?" She showed no appreciation for the fact that these small children had wonderful tone and mature interpretation; her only concern was whether or not they could read notes. Yet I have observed that traditional teaching has not always been successful in teaching reading, either. Sight reading is an art in itself. One must practice to become a good sight reader. One must do a great deal of reading *up to time.*

Whether a child reads in the first years of study or plays by rote and begins a little later has very little to do with his ultimate skill as a sight reader. I doubt that a Suzuki beginning will be a handicap to a student's later efforts to become a good sight reader. When teaching children how to read words we don't insist that he learn to read books while he is learning to talk. Thus the question is: when should the child be taught to read music? The usual reply is, "During the second book, at least for piano." By that time the child should have laid the foundations of his technique and developed much sensitivity. If by this time he still lacks good tone and sensitivity he should not be taught to read. When his attention is absorbed with reading he will forget to produce a good tone and maintain good hand positions, unless these things have become second nature.

Despite this sensible approach to the reading problem on the part of the Suzuki teachers, many people are horrified to learn that children are playing by ear. "Stop!" they cry. "He'll be ruined and never learn to read. Get him to a traditional teacher at once!" The shallowness of this attitude was brought home to me one day in Venezuela, where students are required to take a year of dry theory before they are allowed to touch an instrument. One of the girls visiting our Suzuki Workshop there told me, "My younger sister plays all of the pieces I am working on, but entirely by ear. She is completely bored with her course in theory, and I am afraid that she is going to lose interest in music." The concertmaster of the Symphony told me that many really talented children are stifled by the traditional approach to music. They want to play and lose interest when they are forbidden to in order to learn something that does not seem immediately useful.

Playing by ear is not intended to be an end in itself. It is a beginning. And as Dr. Suzuki has shown, it is one of the most helpful beginnings in the world of musical education.

Chapter 11

When a Violinist Teaches the Cello

Margaret Rowell

"Only now is the cello emerging from its second-place position; it is in the most exciting period of its history."

Although the cello was conceived and born at the same time as the violin, it was quickly overshadowed by its more brilliant relative. The violin at first was considered almost vulgar, for it was compared with the delicate, more feminine viols, with their dulcet tones; but soon its magnificent singing tone and its virtuosity made it the favorite the world over. Every European family longed for one son to become a doctor and another a violinist! We know the result. We have the great schools of violin teaching in Europe and the long line of great violinists.

The cello, the step-brother of the violin, didn't fare as well. It was considered big, clumsy, and not a virtuoso instrument. The viola da gamba, unlike the other viols, remained the preferred instrument: refined, and, because of its frets, capable of rendering music more precisely in tune. Few of the great composers created for the cello as magnificently as they did for the violin.

Bach, however, gave us six remarkable cello suites, which are played more now than they were a hundred years after his death. Mozart did not write any sonatas or concertos for the cello; Mendelssohn and Beethoven wrote sonatas for cello and piano, but no concertos.

Only now is the cello emerging from its second-place position; it is in the most exciting period of its history. It is, in fact, on the verge of a revolution. We are witnessing a kind of Cello Liberation Movement which calls upon us to see the cello, not as an over-sized violin, but as a beautiful stringed instrument, to be considered on its own merits.

Often violin teachers are called upon to teach cello students. Teachers using the Suzuki method particularly, are being asked to help train cellists, for they are naturally intrigued by the method's success with young violinists. For this reason it is important to know the basic differences in the teaching of the two instruments.

VIOLIN

Balance

1. In playing the violin, the balance is through the whole body into the feet, with knees flexible. The weight is transferred from one leg to another. A slight swing of the whole body with central balance is even desirable.

2. The violin has no end pin.

3. The curved large bottom of the violin fits into the neck and body of the player, giving a feeling of security in holding the instrument.

CELLO

Balance

1. In playing the cello, the balance is through a tripod: the seat and the two legs.

   It has taken over 100 years to free ourselves from the "gamba hold," which meant sitting far forward on the chair, and grabbing the cello with both legs, thereby building up tensions.

2. The end pin came in with the beginning of this century. It gave the feeling of security, but has also presented a problem. We have not yet achieved the correct end-pin; like the early bow, it is in transition.

3. The curved large bottom of the cello is away from the player, often slipping with gravity, making the player "grab" the instrument. This difference may be partly responsible for the feeling of clumsiness in holding the cello. Until the instrument is correctly held, it is impossible to get good results.

126

VIOLIN	CELLO
Balance	*Balance*
4. On the violin, the scroll is farthest away from the player's person. The arm is stretched away from the player and the fingers are likewise stretched as they are placed over the finger-board. The arm folds as the fingers fold closer together in ascending into the higher positions.	4. The scroll is closest to the player. The left arm is folded while the fingers are widest apart. As the fingers get closer together (e.g. in going from the first to the other positions), the arm stretches away from the body.
5. In going up the finger-board, the hand is coming towards the player's body; this gives a feeling of security.	5. In going up the finger-board, the hand goes away from the player's body, thus giving a feeling of insecurity.
6. No thumb position.	6. The thumb position is unique for cello and string bass. It is of the utmost importance; all virtuoso music uses it.
7. The bridge curves less than the cello with easier string crossing.	7. The bridge is more curved than the violin bridge, and larger; this demands wider angles in string crossings.
8. The position of the strings in relation to the player are reversed to those of the cello. The E-string, the easiest to play because of its position, is closest to the bow arm.	8. The strings are reversed and the top string is the farthest from the bow arm. The A-string is the most difficult to play; the C-string is easier because of its position in relation to the player's bow arm.
9. The down-bow direction is definitely down; the up-bow goes up.	9. Both down-bow and up-bow do *not* go in those directions, but horizontally. The bow is not held by gravity. the balance is of the utmost importance.

SUZUKI CONCEPT

VIOLIN

Balance

10. The sound comes from the F-holes toward the player, allowing him to hear instantly. The F-holes are on the player's ear level.

11. The bow-hold is very natural, almost like holding a pencil.

12. The little finger is on top of the bow and is used to balance the bow and to cross strings.

13. Relaxed fingers fall from base sockets, allowing the fingers to spread on string without strain.

14. The thumb behind the fingers, and the angle of the finger-board, throws weight forward, giving weight to weak fingers.

CELLO

Balance

10. The sound goes away from the F-holes toward the audience. The player does not hear it instantaneously as does the violinist. The F-holes are not at all on the ear-level of the player.

11. The cello bow is heavier than the violin bow. It has to be held lower and more out in front of the player. The hold on the bow must change from that on the violin in order to accommodate this position.

12. The little finger is held over the bow to give support while crossing the strings. The player crosses strings at a horizontal angle.

13. The fingers strike the string from the side instead of from above. The fingers are more likely to become stiffened. There must also be effort to drop the fingers from the sockets.

14. The cellist cannot place the thumb behind the fingers. It has to balance under the second and third fingers as a fulcrum. The player should allow the full weight to come through each finger.

VIOLIN	CELLO
Balance	*Balance*
15. On the violin it is easy to have equal distance between the fingers. The violin position, with the fingers falling at an angle, allows for natural half and whole steps.	15. A straight position on the cello usually produces 1–23–4, the second and third fingers being close together and unable to play in tune. The cellist has to change the angle of the forearm to correct this and produce equal half steps.
16. The hand can move into positions with more ease. The position change involves less distance for the arm movement and the motion is towards the body. Here too, the arm should transport the hand even on a half-step shift.	16. The aim of the arm is transportation even when moving only a half step. Distances in shifting are greater on the cello. The arm moves away from the body and thus feels less secure.
17. Extensions on the violin are primarily finger movements.	17. Forward extensions on the cello are always combined with an arm movement, moving the thumb with the second finger as a fulcrum.

How then does a violinist teach a cello student? Basically, the two instruments are brothers in the same family of strings and have most of their playing and problems in common.

How should we start a cello student so that he may achieve a relaxed, easy hold of his cello? Here are just a few suggestions:

1) Tripod balance (seat and two feet).
2) Ability to "spring up" in "one piece."
3) Put hands on knees and feel suction fingers, with flow-through from the back as center, not from the upper arm only. Watch a pianist!

4) "Bear hug!" Let the student fold his arms across the body of the cello, be able to get up and walk around with it, always with supple arms and suction fingers.

5) Sit while still holding the cello with the "bear hug," adjust end pin to correct height.

6) Let the cello rest against the right knee, exposing the full left side of the instrument. Then gently let the left knee cling to the underside of the cello. Be able to move it back and forth with supple knees. Have end pin solidly in the floor.

7) Clasp the hands across the front of the cello and try to pull apart. Then get the feel of the same suction hands, while doing pizzicato of both left and right hand.

8) Transfer this feeling to center balance hold of bow.

9) Transfer this feeling to left hand as it goes up entire length of fingerboard; first, between the strings, using them as railroad tracks, later, on the string, with bow playing tremolo.

10) Before playing the first position, be sure the student is able to reach any part of the fingerboard—all registers, all strings—with the left hand, and use the entire length of the bow with the right hand (even though the player starts at the middle).

11) The body is the fulcrum (like a see-saw). The arms are light and free to move at all times.

With this very brief introduction, the violinist should be able to adapt and understand the cello, and teach it with the same basic principles as the violin.

We need you, violinists, to help us! I hope this gives a little enlightenment on the beginnings of cello instruction.

Chapter 12

Teaching Suzuki in a Public School System

Diana Tillson

". . . I can state unequivocally that I would never return to traditional string class teaching."

How effective is the Suzuki concept in a public school system? Its merits are best demonstrated by contrasting students who have been trained by traditional string class methods and materials with students developed through a Suzuki class approach. After directing a Suzuki-oriented string program in Bedford, New York, for more than seven years, I can state unequivocally that I would never return to traditional string class teaching. The Suzuki concept, I venture to suggest, has affected the public school string class even more profoundly than it has the private violin studio.

That is not to say that we have no problems in our Suzuki-oriented classes. We do. After outlining the program in our school system I will describe both the joys and hazards that we have encountered.

Our school system is in Westchester County, about two hours north of New York City, in a suburban area with a fortunate admixture of social and economic levels. We have five elementary schools, a middle school, and a senior high school. We begin to teach the violin in the first grade in each of our elementary schools.

1st Grade Level—Preparatory Violin Program

To introduce the program to students and parents we offer a

131

six to ten weeks exploratory course which meets in large groups two or three times each week. All except working parents are required to attend these sessions, where a variety of activities gives an understanding of what the future program will be like. Materials used are cardboard boxes and bowsticks. Activities include directed listening to the "Twinkle Variations" with speech rhythms, bowing eurhythmics, clapping, and singing, as well as games designed to teach posture, bowing, and fingering. Upon completion of the exploratory program parents attend an orientation session. There they and the faculty discuss the Suzuki Talent Education philosophy and the modifications necessary to its application to a public school program. We ask our school library to circulate among the parents copies of Dr. Suzuki's book, "Nurtured by Love."

At this point some families will have decided not to continue with the school's program. The parent may be unable to give the time; the child's initial curiosity and present interest may have been satisfied; the child may have become discouraged by the demands of motor coordination, sustained concentrated attention, or group discipline. Lastly, we may recommend that the child is not yet ready to profit from class, as opposed to individual, instruction. Invariably these families are most appreciative of their short-term experience in the preparatory program.

1st Grade Level—Beginning Violin Classes

Those students who are now ready to enter the first year of our formal program are scheduled for two 15-minute lessons each week in classes of two, with parents in attendance. If a parent works and cannot attend and has been unable to procure a substitute parent on a regular basis (such as a relative or neighbor) his child is scheduled for three 15-minute lessons weekly in classes of two. Parents rent violins from the school at a cost of $15 a year; they must purchase Suzuki Violin Book I and Record I–II. The child who has no parent in attendance at lessons is not permitted to take his violin home until the "Twinkle Variations" have been mastered, unless practicing can be supervised by someone with Suzuki training (an older brother or sister, perhaps).

2nd Grade Level

Continuing students are scheduled for two 20-minute lessons a week in classes of three students. The attendance of parents is still required. Children of working parents take three lessons weekly. Beginning second grade students are assimilated into first grade classes.

3rd–5th Grade Level

Continuing students are scheduled for two 30-minute lessons a week in larger groups (with maximum class size of six students). The attendance of parents is encouraged at the third-grade level, but is optional thereafter. A beginning violin section is offered each year to students from grades 3–5 who seemed not ready when younger, and to new transfer students.

Students who transfer into the district after beginning violin study elsewhere are helped to accommodate to our Suzuki classes. Just as we hesitate to accept into our program children whose parents cannot attend lessons, so are we reluctant to start older beginners, for we know these students will be denied many of the benefits inherent in the Suzuki philosophy. Yet as a public school system we must serve all our children. If we reject a child we are bound to create an enemy of the schools.

Middle School Level, Grades 6–8

String students are scheduled for five 40-minute instructional classes every two weeks, with a class size of six to ten students. In addition, all string players have three orchestra rehearsals a week: a sectional rehearsal (30 minutes), string orchestra (30 minutes), full orchestra with winds and percussion (70 minutes).

High School Level, Grades 9–12

String students are scheduled daily for orchestra, which carries a full unit of credit. Chamber music ensembles are built into the daily orchestra schedule. All students are offered one additional instructional class period weekly. At this level we strongly encourage private study outside of school, as well as membership in local youth orchestras, inter-school and all-state festivals.

Qualified students are given the opportunity to perform solo literature with orchestral accompaniment (such as Saint-Saens: Cello Concerto, Mozart: Symphonie Concertante for Violin-Viola). The high school orchestra also provides accompaniments for group performances of the younger students in the following Suzuki repertoire:

Bach: Minuets
Beethoven: Minuet in G
Boccherini: Minuet
Bach: Gavotte; Suite #3
Seitz: Concerto movements
Vivaldi: Concerto movements
Bach: Double Concerto
Fiocco: Allegro

Viola, Cello, String Bass Program

In our school district all string instruction is of homogeneous groups. The cello program begins at the 4th–5th grade level, utilizing our own repertory sequence of cello literature with books and recordings supplied to the students. We plan to start cello instruction much younger as we acquire smaller cellos.

The viola and string bass programs begin at the middle school level. Viola students usually are experienced violinists, who will have accomplished enough in that area to make rapid progress in the new one. Bass and viola students go quickly through the Suzuki-Zahtilla Book I, then concentrate on standard instructional materials to prepare for orchestra and ensemble participation.

Reading Program

From the very first lessons we prepare students for music-reading. In Grades 1 and 2 we play reading readiness games. We do rote singing of the folksongs in Book I, using speech patterns, texts, Kodály time names, note names, and bowings. We explore the staff by steps and skips on the floor with voice and hand. We emphasize aural and tactile recognition of whole steps and half steps, relating the note names to the violin fingerboard. We teach phrase recognition by rote. Even at this early age it is possible to read and write the notes of the open strings on the staff.

By Grades 3–5 the children are reading music. All reading readiness techniques are applied to notation and to the music score. Ear training is continued. The children are reading simple duet parts to the Book I folksongs. At first this is tonal reading only, as the rhythm parallels the first violin part.

Reading material must be structured as carefully for rhythmic content as for tonality. At this level a substantial proportion of the students' reading material is correlated with their general vocal music class activities.

By Grades 6–8, we undertake the formal study of key signatures and time signatures, scales and arpeggios. Reading materials include:

Matesky & McMasters: Finger Families for Orchestra (Highland)
Whistler & Hummel: Scales & Bowings, 3 vol. (Rubank)
Blumberg: Practical Violin Method (Editions Musicales)
Hrimaly: Scales for Violin (Schirmer)
Klengel: Technical Studies for Cello (Schirmer)
Suzuki: Position Etudes (Zen-On)
Preston: Direct Approach to Higher Positions for String Classes (Belwin)
Suzuki: Duet Materials (Summy-Birchard)
Applebaum: Duets for Strings (Belwin)
Applebaum: Beautiful Music for Two String Instruments, 4 vol. (Belwin)
Gearhart & Green: Fiddle Sessions (Shawnee)
Arnond & Alshin: Easy Ensembles for Cello & Base (A M P)

Doflein: Method for Violin, 4 vol. (Schott) Duet materials.

Feuillard: Methode du Jeune Violoncelliste, 6 vol. (Galaxy) Duet materials.

Bartok: Duets for Two Violins; Duets for Two Cellos (Boosey & Hawkes)

An Evaluation

Here, then, is my comparison of the Bedford Suzuki-oriented string program with a traditional public school string program where the school instruction is not supplemented by private study:

1) Performing technique can be developed earlier and to a much higher level, notably intonation, left hand speed and accuracy, bowing reflexes, tone production, left-right hand coordination, speed and security of tonal memory, and playing posture.

2) Solo as well as ensemble literature can be studied in depth.

3) Reading skills can be equivalent, if a reading program is structured from the very start.

4) Drop-out rate is greatly reduced.

And this is how I compare our program with private studio instruction:

1) Progress will always be slower in group instruction, but the quality of work or standard of playing can be nearly as fine.

2) Motivation is often stronger.

3) Orchestra and ensemble experience are an advantage.

We do face recurrent problems: the development and training of staff, administrative support, financing, scheduling, the right amount of parent participation, and good communication between school, home, and community.

We have developed our Suzuki program very gradually over an eight-year period and find that its greatest strength lies in its district-wide continuum, from first through eighth grade. Yet we can never relax our vigilance; we can never take for granted that the program is permanently assured. We must continually rebuild administrative and community support.

Our students are our greatest allies. Dr. Suzuki has pointed them toward habits of excellence and has given them the means of achieving excellence, an idealism with strong appeal to the young people of today. It is for us to help them secure it.

Europe taught us that a precocious child is born in a special environment, that his father plays in the Berlin Philharmonic and his ancestors have always been musicians . . . .

America came along and said, "We want everybody to have a chance to hold every instrument of the orchestra." And so we have these terrible things going on in the name of music education. But don't forget that we were the first to say that we want to give music to everyone.

And then our dear Dr. Suzuki came along and said, "Yes, you're right. Everyone should have that opportunity. But if you will control that home environment, if you will control that teaching environment, if you will work through the child's natural abilities to learn as he has a natural ability to eat or to learn his mother tongue, then you will do a better job for America than you are now doing in the public school system.

Europe is still shaking its head over both of us. A whole class of European trained or European thinking musicians despairs. It's a little like religions, because we're all a little that way. The fundamentalist religion will very often exclude you because you're bound for hell. The liberal, creedless religion includes everybody. Well, something in between is the best. We, while trying to use Dr. Suzuki's ideas, also have ourselves tuned to the European idea. If we accomplish the goals of both musical excellence and musical democracy, we have done the very best for our children.

Yvonne Tait

Chapter 13

To Parents Concerned About Music Reading

Elizabeth Mills

"As traditionally taught, a small minority became really fine readers, and the rest ranged from fair to poor."

"But can they read music?" is a question many people ask the teachers after hearing young Suzuki instrumentalists play a difficult piece beautifully. They show concern and a basic distrust of playing by ear or rote. Much poor reading among musical children has always been blamed on their ability to play by ear. While even children who speak well may have word-reading difficulties, I have never heard anyone question whether it was possible that learning to talk interfered with the process of learning to read!

In both instances, reading is a separate skill, though related both to speaking and playing. The music-reading ability of the advanced Suzuki players varies, just as word-reading ability would among children who speak fluently and well. Reading problems have many sources, but they are not caused by talking or playing first. Correct concepts, motivation, practice, and freedom from impairing physiological or psychological factors are all basic pre-conditions to the development of the highest quality of reading skill, and will be discussed again later.

I am glad people have concern about reading, for it is an important aspect of the complete musical experience, and one in which the parent can either help or hinder. *Teachers and parents must work together to help students hear musically, and then read in a completely musical way.*

138

I feel that the child who has learned to hear and to play musically is the most likely candidate for the *complete* reader. By that I mean that when he reads new music for the first time, quite automatically he will try to hear it in his mind. He will look not only for the note and its duration, but for the expressive and stylistic clues like pedaling, bowing, dynamics, textures (like *staccato*), phrasing, and tempo, as well as signs of form (like repeat marks, *D.C.* and *Fine.*) The music will come alive fairly quickly instead of sounding dull and meaningless. Too many of us teachers have spent years scolding children who constantly forgot to notice, or even remember what it meant when they saw such terms as *dolce, grazioso,* and *leggiero.*

Unfortunately, it is typical to teach reading principally by drilling on note *names,* with some agonizing counting thrown in, of course. The musical results are similar to what they are in word reading when a child has been drilled on alphabet recognition to the point that the alphabet is all he sees when he comes to a word. He sees individual letters but doesn't hear the word in his mind, thus "getting the message." He can say "it's a half note" when queried about the kind of a note that he missed, but he didn't *feel* two beats.

A much higher proportion of the American Suzuki students who have reached Book 5 level of violin work, in my experience, seem to be approaching the *complete reader* level than was true of violin students at that technical level ten years ago—students who had, of course, been taught more traditionally. Those who are motivated to read, at an appropriate stage, do so with ease. When tested by being asked to look at unfamiliar phrases of music completely out of context (to make it harder to guess how they might sound), students at the Book 4 and 5 levels have in almost all cases *sung* the material with correct rhythm and phrasing, on the exact pitches indicated in the music and without help of any kind. This included "difficult" keys like E^b, chromatic signs like extra sharps and flats, and bowings that might trip them in phrasing. They did not use their instruments as tools to find out mechanically how it would sound, and thus proved that the musical codes had given them a musical message.

Whether such students can *play* equally well reading music will depend in large part on whether the music is of a type and level with which they have had previous experience so that their physical reflexes can enter in. Again, it is much like word reading. One's speaking ability moves ahead of one's reading ability until one reaches a fairly advanced stage of education.

When these students participate regularly in some type of ensemble which provides motivation and practice in reading under pressure, they extend their ability to read rapidly. As with all other abilities, reading ability when used creates more reading ability. To understand clearly why it seems best to postpone its development when it is such an important ability later, I wish to go extensively into the drawbacks of early reading.

Reading Creates Many Obstacles

Reading is usually thought of as indispensable to the learning of new music, but it can also be a great obstacle to the development of even more important musical abilities. It is a part of the music education process which merits re-thinking and re-structuring. The obstacles occur most frequently when a student approaches reading and learning to play an instrument at the same time. It seems best either to learn to read while using the voice only—as in the approach of Zoltan Kodaly—or to learn to make music on an instrument and then proceed to learn to read, as in the approach of Suzuki.

It is to be hoped, for the good of all children, not just those fortunate enough to study privately, that Kodaly's contribution, with its great success in Hungary, may be adapted on a wide scale in American schools with equal success. Many years ago it was standard practice in American elementary schools to take a step toward musical literacy by sight-singing songs using the *do, re, mi* syllables. This practice disappeared because, as used, it robbed children of the zest and esthetic experience music should provide. It was too mechanical. Kodaly has shown ways that this need not be so, just as Suzuki has shown how to provide the student with the ability to play an instrument well with pleasure, and yet without sacrificing ultimate comprehensive musicianship.

Whether the child does learn to read well will depend especially upon how well the parent understands the process of *learning* to read music, and is helped by the teacher to follow a good plan that does not introduce obstacles. Many parents, of course, know how to read music already to some degree, but this does not mean they can teach their children easily. They must, like the teacher, think through the whole reading subject carefully and proceed with an understanding of the learning process. On the other hand, the parent who learns to read music in order to help his child may have some advantages, for he learns first the very things that will help his child learn when it is time.

An Obstacle to Enjoyment

Music reading became an obstacle to enjoyment in the situation referred to in the elementary use of reading by syllables. One very important truth to remember is that children and older beginning music students, too, can sing, play and compose music more difficult than they can read or notate. Why deprive them of that pleasure? With what zest they play music that sounds like real music, not "baby stuff." Think for a moment of the thrill shown by the child who has learned to play "Chop Sticks." He can't leave it alone. It isn't the music *alone*. It is the way he learned it that freed him to play in such a way that he could make it sound like something. He can play it with facility and speed, rhythm, and even good tone quality *if* he originally heard it played with good tone quality. No one has to tell him to practice it!

Dr. Suzuki solves the problem of the usual early boredom by avoiding music simple enough for the beginner to read, and by letting him hear it on records. A four-line piece of music certainly can sound more impressive than it looks. He chose pieces of solid musical quality, playable by the beginner but with both musical and instrumental challenges which provide all the meat for practice. Most of the necessary exercise and technical material are then extracted—and *this is essential*—directly from the literature. The student understands this better than he can the remote needs which generate the production of the usual technical books for the early years.

An Obstacle to Musical Memory Development

Among the abilities blocked by early dependence on reading is that of a dependable memory. It is a well known fact in the music profession that the best readers usually have the most difficulty memorizing. Because children who learn music without the help of the printed page are forced to remember what they have worked out, and because this means they must analyze to remember, memory is no problem. They take note of the form of the music by finding similarities, differences, and repetitions in the *sound*. The pieces are fully absorbed, and with enough use, just as in the use of vocabulary, they remain readily accessible. When music becomes part of one's brain cells instead of remaining on the printed page to be turned into music by an habitual eye-to-finger response, the student usually builds up a large repertoire of music to which he turns for emotional outlet. Musicianship and understanding of the instrument are strengthened at the same time.

An Obstacle to Fine Technical Control

When a student plays through most of his practice time while staring at music on a rack, deeply engrossed in decoding those black marks, he seldom has fine technical control of his physical "tools." Let us remember that there are several codes: for pitch, rhythm, fingering, bowing, breathing, pedaling, form, and expression. They are all used simultaneously, and add to the perceptual complexity caused by the five staff lines which must be read from left to right and up and down at the same time making it even more difficult than reading a complex sentence like this one. How can the student look at his hands and arms and control his motions within a rhythmic framework, so that the desired sounds are produced, while he needs to look at music to find out what to play next? In the case of piano, he either stumbles along in the music while looking down, or makes inferior motions while looking up, or loses his place while looking back and forth, up and down.

In Dr. Suzuki's work, the technical control begins immediately, especially so far as tone work. *Tonalization* is the term he has introduced and which he uses constantly. In addition to some specific short exercises for violinists, *tonalization is a way of working* on the full range of technical needs. It operates to improve the sound of every type of passage. Who wants to listen to thin, squeaky tones when hearing either a beginner's "Twinkle" or an advanced player's Paganini?

An Obstacle to Pitch and Tempo Senses

The maintaining of a steady tempo, and the development of accurate pitch production also fall victims to the common reading procedures. To control pitch and tempo, one must hear oneself realistically and very consciously in order to compare the actual sound with the intended sound. But the brain simply does not tune into the messages from the ear when paying attention primarily to those coming from the page to the eye. The habit of listening to pitch and responding to the inner rhythmic sense is difficult to develop if one spends most of one's playing time reading. This is true throughout a musician's life.

An Obstacle to Listening to Other Members of a Musical Team

When one accompanies a soloist or a group, or plays in an ensemble or orchestra, a vital requirement is that one must listen to the others and relate one's own part to theirs in an appropriate manner. This is greatly hampered if reading is difficult. This suggests two possibilities: postpone that type of experience, or help the student learn to read well, although other aspects of his playing may suffer and the ensemble's sound suffers as well. Since the evidence is against the latter course, let us keep in mind the need to bring about the right conditions so that he may be reading well when he reaches the age when he would thoroughly enjoy the ensemble experience—usually in one's teens.

The desire to play with others is increased by the group playing experience in Suzuki programs, at least in the case of orchestral instruments. When the habit of hearing his own sound is well established, the student will find a powerful incentive to read and plenty of reading practice by joining an orchestra or smaller ensemble.

At this point, speed-reading should be studied most seriously. In the manual on reading which Dr. Suzuki published in Japan, there are progressively shorter time limits set on the completion of work-book type exercises, ranging from 90 seconds down to 15 seconds per line of similar material. It is a book that has many interesting concepts of presentation different from most American texts, but unfortunately it is available only in the Japanese language.

An Obstacle to Artistry

The saddest loss caused by premature emphasis on reading is that of musically artistic and meaningful performance. An essential, and most unconscious part of any reading experience is what we usually refer to as "reading *between* the lines." Much of the meaning in speech is conveyed, not by the word itself but, by the tone, pitch, loudness, and timing with which it is uttered. It is impossible to put this on paper. One can pronounce, "I like that," in so many ways that it may mean any of a number of things. One might say *"I* like that.", "I *like* that!", "I like *that.*", or finally, *"I like that!"*, the latter meaning the exact reverse of what it appears on paper. What neophyte actor, never having heard Shakespeare, could be expected to read Shakespeare lines properly? Or, taking the

144

case of foreign language, who would expect to speak correctly by studying mainly the written language? So it is with music. The inflection and nuance *cannot be written* but it *can be imitated.* The answer, of course, is to hear and experience extensively both specific pieces of music and enough examples of each musical style. Then the printed page becomes a series of hints which evoke one's own experiences.

Appreciation of Music Notation

The list of obstacles is not intended to underplay the importance of the printed note, but to bring out the damage done when the teaching of reading is not worked into a comprehensively balanced plan. It should lead to high and satisfying levels of playing skill, musical knowledge and literacy, and artistic expression.

The needed musical know-how for today's players is very complex, for we continue to play the music of all the periods for which there is written music. We must know the main facts about notation and musical customs from at least the time of Corelli—the mid-seventeenth century—to the present. We must have a *sense* of history, and also a fair *knowledge of details* about techniques used, rhythmic practices, and styles of playing. We must know the formal structures used, whether in the dance music or in the larger sonata forms. We must have a keen sense of the differences in scales commonly used and the harmonic progressions.

Our children growing up through music—first hearing, then playing and later reading—learn some of this through their ears. They later find that reading the facts in notation clarifies what they have heard. From the dawn of Man's history to the medieval period, *music existed without notation* except for the rudest forms. People learned to sing and play instruments without standing in front of music racks reading exercises, scales and etudes. They were undoubtedly drawn to the most musical and expressive singers and instrumentalists from whom they learned by imitation and direct help.

Some of these player-teachers, during the fifteenth to eighteenth centuries, were probably able to use the developing notational system to jot down a little music at lessons to help their pupils remember the outline of the music they had just learned, but memory was the ability they depended upon the most in those days. Printed *beginners' books* were definitely not given out, for they did not exist until music-printing became less expensive and consequently more common—and that was about the middle of the eighteenth century. A composer like Bach would write down tuneful minuets and other popular dances of the day in little notebooks for his children or pupils. The child would hear the pieces composed and see the notebooks grow, and would thus understand that being a player was synonomous with being able to make up music and write it down.

Musical creativity in both teacher and pupil was a natural by-product of this earlier type of learning. It sometimes has been pointed out that Bach, Handel, Vivaldi and others of that period were not as remarkable as the level of culture from which they rose. They were like the highest peaks of a tremendous mountain range that is even more remarkable than its individual high peaks.

It well might be that the tremendous creative vitality of that time was due in part to an unusual combination of circumstances: the musicians all had a degree of creativity which stemmed from the direct and natural way of learning music from another musician without depending upon a beginners' book. At the same time they could take advantage of the notation system which permitted the logical development of ideas and extended compositions beyond previous limits. Those composers had a unique combination of circumstances.

The course of music history changed in an important respect after 1800, and I suspect that the type of beginners' manuals that had emerged from publishers for the first time may have been a root cause. While any musician living in the eighteenth century could improvise cadenzas and many other musical forms, this inventive ability gradually died out. The typical student was no longer creative. He had lost the instinct to compose his own music—an ability which had been standard in previous generations. Composing became a specialty in the music field, and has remained so ever since.

Since I began to use Dr. Suzuki's ideas, one of the surprises which has been a delight to me has been the number of young students who just naturally create their own music without any suggestion from an adult. "I made up a new piece last night," has been the opening statement at many, many lessons. When I ask, "Can you play it for me?", the response is an indignant, "Well, of course!" Mothers report that the music played for me does indeed sound like what they heard at home the night before. (An instance of memory developing—including also, the mother's memory.) Many of the melodies have been constructed, of course, out of a vocabulary of rhythms and note patterns used in the repertory. Others are quite original. Some children make up endless variations on "Twinkle"—note variations with ornaments, rhythm variations, and minor and other harmonic variations. One child at the level of the Bach Minuets improvised at her lesson each week a cadenza at the end of Suzuki's "Perpetual Motion," playing long flights of note patterns up and down the fingerboard, all different each week. This is how it seems to start. I have seen it develop into group improvisation with two or three students playing together and taking turns in leading off with a motif, as in the type of work developed by Carl Orff. Many of the creative expressions are carried over to the piano or a recorder or other instrument by the young violinists.

From what I am seeing rather commonly, I think it is possible that we can again have a period when large numbers of young people will grow up fully at home on several instruments —composing and performing, and doing it well. This will be a way of life for them and their friends—an outlet that will spill over into their social and home life regardless of their professions. What a cultural base for the future!

Comparison of Learning to Read Words and Music

In helping a student learn to *read* music, not just play it by ear and imitation, teachers and the guiding parents should take note again and again from the ways in which children learn to *talk*. Dr. Suzuki was most astute in calling the world's attention to the *overlooked importance of Man's universal success in learning speech.* Overlooked it has been because it has been assumed wrongly that speech ability apparently is built into each person, while other abilities like music, reasoning, mechanics, and painting are special ones appearing genetically in a smaller portion of the population.

Dr. Suzuki's work is widely known so far as his application of the successful speech methods to helping countless children play the violin as fluently as they speak even though they were taught without having been screened for "talent." Less well known are his efforts to help teachers of many subjects outside of music to develop high abilities in the very young.

We must not compound our educational failures by failing to make further applications of his insights. We should now see where we can go by applying them to reading. This whole subject is loaded with emotion because Man has *not* had universal success in teaching reading and writing, whether in literature or in music! Countless methods of teaching have been devised throughout the history of the written word. Everywhere, an elite minority of successful scholars developed, while another part of the population could read only adequately, and a distressingly large part were illiterate. One of the dreams of most modern societies has been to make every man literate, but while literacy figures look high in many statistics, we hear the term *functional illiterate* often enough to remind us that we haven't succeeded as we have in speech. In music it is the same thing. As traditionally taught, a small minority become really fine readers and the rest range from fair to poor. It is easy to see, then, why so many music teachers are fearful that Suzuki-oriented students will not learn to read—they are having so much trouble with tradi-

148

tional teaching producing a high enough rate of excellence in music-reading. I can see many ways which indicate that we have a better chance with our students who do not try to combine instrumental and reading skills at the beginning, but who do spend time becoming musical first.

Does Man have trouble with reading because he has not evolved far enough for his requisite perceptual abilities or predisposition to read to become equal to his hearing abilities? This just could not be the answer for Man seems, in reality, to have stronger visual orientation than aural. Dr. Glenn Doman, in the first chapter of *How to Teach Your Baby to Read,* indicates his belief that infants could learn to read even before talking if we wished them to and used the proper method of stimulation at the right time.

The age range factor is one clue to be followed in analyzing Man's success with speech. The infant himself seems to control this, for no matter how much the parent feels he should be ready to talk and how much the home environment is providing stimulus, it is the infant's own neurological time table that allows him to respond. The environment is certainly the determining factor, though, in *how* he will talk, for a baby does not inherit a specific language genetically. A Japanese baby growing up in another language environment and hearing no Japanese will certainly not speak Japanese.

Pre-language Communication

Another set of clues that we must follow as guides to success, in guiding a child through the stages of learning to read, lies in the *customary sequence* of stages in learning to speak. First there is pre-language communication, during which the baby begins to note and associate changes in voice levels of pitch and loudness with emotional states. He develops a perfect memory of his mother's voice—especially its pitch—when she is tired, anxious, happy, or jubilant. Next comes increased attention to speech and much listening practice over many months while the brain is organizing sounds into meaningful units, and nerve pathways are developing which will permit the infant to respond vocally by imitation. He has been making an increased variety of experimental sounds to accomplish this. (Applying this to music, not only playing for an infant, but being with him and responding emotionally to the music will start him on the road to using music as an outlet and form of communication.)

During the period until he has a vocabulary of two or three thousand words, he will pay more *conscious* attention to tone quality and pitch than he ever will again in getting verbal messages from his family. This must be the reason why considerable musical experience before age five has been shown to produce the best chance of his learning to name notes by pitch—referred to as absolute pitch or pitch recognition.

About the time the infant is "vocalizing" near enough to the correct sounds to be ready for speaking, those in his environment begin to choose just a few words relating to things which have meaning to the infant, speaking them more loudly and clearly than in normal sentences. (We can choose music the young player already has learned and likes, and we can put some of the notes on cards to enlarge them.) We repeat those words frequently. (Ditto the symbol cards.) We also speak with a full range of expressive nuance, or else the child will learn to repeat words without infusing them with the meaning given by voice quality, pitch, and emphasis. (Play recordings by the finest artists.) When the child succeeds in imitating a word, he is rewarded with smiles, hugs, laughter, and all sorts of pleasant actions. Then there is repetition before a new word is added. (Recognize and reward the achievement of a small musical step and make the most of it before insisting on another.) The larger his vocabulary grows, of course, the more quickly his experience permits him to pick up a new word.

We listen to him using words and we glory in his development without ever saying, "Now you must begin to practice speaking one hour a day." (Why do we say that in music?)

We find that we must let him speak without constant corrections and testing or he will become stubborn and not reward us with further practice and growth in speech. (Ditto in playing and reading music!) Rather than calling attention to all his shortcomings and mistakes of pronunciation, *we* keep using the problem words in a patient and friendly way so that he can hear the correct model repeated for weeks and months if necessary. We use words with similar sounds, too. Finally, he will manage one day to say the problem sound correctly and with the pride of *self-correction*. (In music there are similar ways, when a child is playing or reading music poorly, to provide models which do not rob him of thinking for himself and yet assure him that we are "on his team" while he works toward the correct performance.) We must seek continuously for methods parallel to our successful ways in helping speech develop, not only in music but for all types of reading—mainly because it is a simple, natural, and therefore, comfortable process for a child.

Effects of the Type of Musical Activity on Music Reading

In addition to thinking about the various stages in acquiring basic speaking skills I want to touch on the much later variety of uses of the written language which determine the mental approach to reading for each of the uses. After acquiring considerable skill in reading, we do not necessarily aim for accurate reading. In language, it depends upon the uses to which we put the material, whether we read and re-read slowly and carefully, paying attention to every comma in order to understand precisely what is meant. We may read rapidly and superficially for pleasure. We may skim through a newspaper. We may memorize facts for a test. We may struggle with a foreign language. We may struggle with a special vocabulary for a special field like medicine, philosophy, or anthropology. None of us is a competent reader in every field because of the special vocabularies and differences in thought processes. No one expects us to be.

This is just as true in musical experience. In preparing students for all the contingencies of music reading, it takes many years. A big question, therefore, is, for which situations should we prepare students and at what stage? How well should they play before they enter orchestra so that they can respond instantly to the messages of their eyes without getting horribly tense? After all, they must meet the pressures of sight-reading at the speed of the conductor's baton. In this situation, it should be noted, skimming is required not complete note accuracy.

In reading to learn a new solo which has not been heard previously, we read much more slowly in order to establish complete accuracy. In this case, we are not usually under pressure to read at another person's rate. Closer analysis of musical structure corresponds to the lawyer's analysis of grammar and punctuation. The more one learns about *musical* grammar or theory, the better one can decode a complex piece harmonically, and bring out the structure of the composition in playing. This is especially important when one is striving to develop a unique interpretation.

In music, as in language, we have the problem of specialized forms of notation and "vocabulary" for different composers and different historical periods. Three or four times each century, enough changes have occurred in playing styles and practices to offer players challenges in understanding the notation. If one attempts to learn music of an unfamiliar style without having heard it or similar music, the performance will leave much out. In trying to play *popular* music, for example, the person whose whole music-reading experience has been related to so-called *classical* music will find little help from the printed page. He must have listened carefully to the style and have absorbed certain musical customs. For example, he must learn that to play what looks like a series of equal *eighth notes,* he must make them unequal! They must have a swinging ratio of 2:1. Or, to give another example, in jumping back to a page of music published in 1700, he must learn to add to the printed page the missing ornaments and flourishes—left to the discretion of each player—and that is no small task. If he gets involved in reading music written in 1890, he must face the constantly changing key signatures and the hundreds of extra sharps, flats, and naturals which indicate the complex harmonic system then in use.

We have here another comparison with language needs. We must eventually speak in and read foreign languages to be highly educated. Let us not expect too much of our students too soon, though. If they have a limited amount of experience in the various types of musical activity, gaining at least the concepts of how to approach the problems, they will be able to return at a later age and broaden their skills and understanding if a new field opens up.

At different periods in a person's study, and in his later life, too, only one or two of these uses or approaches to reading will predominate at a given time. Amateur or professional, one must be a *very* active and really versatile musician to be using them all. When one does change roles musically, one must expect to do intensive work to develop skill adequate to the particular area of activity if new to it. The reading demands vary widely for accompanists, soloists, chamber music or symphony players, commercial work like television and movies, composers, conductors, and musicologists. If one understands the reading process, the playing process, and the musical process, one's amazing human powers of adaptation will permit one to develop the requisite abilities.

The Importance of Reading Does Not Diminish the Playing Priority

Most parents are well aware of the controversies over early reading, which are occurring with increasing frequency, in part due to television commercials and their methods (take note!) and to "Sesame Street." The opposition of many educators and psychologists to early reading is usually due to the frequent and damaging pressures from adults, confusion on entering school, and the fact that reading is a "splinter skill" which does not stimulate enough of the child's nervous system at the age when maturing down to the finger tips and toes is important. (I might worry if a child spent hours a day reading and had no activities involving muscles.) There are, however, many school teachers and a number of neurologists who are very enthusiastic about three-year-olds playing the violin or another instrument in the Suzuki manner. They realize the complete challenge to mind, muscles and nerves; to sensitivity to touch, motion, hearing, and sight. On top of all that, they realize that it provides tools for expression of spirit and emotion. Early reading, though, has many things to recommend it, and there is no question but what the children themselves, usually enjoy it thoroughly. I witnessed this in the pre-school division of the Talent Education Institute in Matsumoto. There I witnessed 3-, 4-, and 5-year-old children learning to read the difficult characters borrowed from Chinese calligraphy. Since word reading, in English at least, is considerably simpler than music reading, there is no doubt that it can be approached earlier.

But still, for all the reasons given so far, I believe with Dr. Suzuki that music-reading is an experience to postpone. Experience with spoken language still precedes reading, except in the presence of abnormalities. The wisdom of this transcends the matter of skills with which we have been concerned thus far. The wisdom of it stems from the purpose of language, (both verbal and musical): communication between people— direct, immediate communication! In a sense, the verbal language by which we communicate facts, ideas and needs, and the musical language by which we communicate the whole gamut of human emotions with considerable precision, are really one. It is our need to relate directly to one another which prompts us to put speaking before reading. Before embarking on the use of symbols *representing* someone's musical communication, we need to sing and play to one another directly.

GUIDE-LINE SUMMARY FOR THE MUSIC-READING EXPERIENCE

I   Music is for the ear, not the eye, and therefore should be experienced thoroughly and consciously before its symbols are introduced.

Throughout the development of playing and reading ability, parallels should be found and used from the sequence normally found in the learning of the spoken language.

II   The time is ripe for learning to read music when the following conditions have been met:

- Good posture in relation to the instrument has developed to the point where it is maintained with a minimum of reminding.
- Technical motions are basically free, secure and correct.
- Musical sensitivity is shown in matters of tone, pitch, and rhythm.
- Musical memory and alertness of observation combine to permit accurate imitation.
- The neurological development is mature enough to permit success in meeting the reading demands without seriously impairing the musical and technical abilities which have been developed.
- A need for reading exists, e.g., when a level of difficulty is reached (most probably during Book 4 in the case of violin) when the parent-teacher can no longer assist sufficiently in calling out fingering and bowing instructions to insure accuracy, or when orchestra experience is just ahead.
- Interest in reading and a curiosity about the symbols exist. (If a young child lives in a home where he sees older people reading, this may be present very early. A little play-acting may be necessary to satisfy him. In cases where need exists but interest is not present, if all other conditions have been met the teacher must effectively stimulate interest.)

III   Maintenance of listening habits for tone, pitch, and expressive qualities is possible if a large proportion of a day's playing time is done from memory, or at least in a manner where the student glances at the music briefly for information and immediately looks back at his playing (or closes his eyes to listen), alternating the two modes.

This is just as true for professionals and advanced students as for beginning readers. The brain, otherwise, pays more attention to seeing ahead than to evaluating the sounds reported by the ear.

IV   A student should continue to perform by memory at lessons after reaching the reading stage, thus being better able to control the musical and technical matters.

Exceptions would be when working on reading skills, and, of course, when referring to and marking points in the music where the learning is inaccurate. This would follow the performance of music prepared for the lesson. (In the case of students under ten, the parent is more efficient in marking music, but the student should be drawn into the process by watching.)

The length of time before *all* of the conditions listed under item II are actually present will vary from one to three or more years. It will depend upon the age when study begins, the student's degrees of concentration and coordination, the difficulty of his instrument, the degree of musicality already developed when study began, the nature of that musicality as related to the instrument (pitch sense is obviously more needed by a violinist than a pianist), and whether the student is emotionally comfortable in the music situation at home, in the studio, and at school.

In any case, reading should never be pushed at a time when a child is emotional over other learning problems. Practical considerations which differ from one student to another often lead teachers and parents to compromise and start a student learning new music by a reading approach when one or more of the above-listed conditions is still weak. The best development of the full spectrum of musicality, technical skill, and literacy, however, is more likely when the full list of conditions is met. The younger the student is when he begins to study, the more likely that will be.

The skillful reading of music is aided by prior physical development. Here, Sister Therese Cecile Murphy demonstrates the need for coordination.

Chapter 14

Practical Suggestions for Teachers on Reading

Harlow and Elizabeth Mills

"Much of the worry over reading may be caused by lack of clear analysis . . ."

Dr. Suzuki has made a major contribution to the teaching of reading by *deferring* it. This has forced us to re-think and re-structure the development of the various abilities connected with music reading, as well as of the more academic aspects of becoming a complete musician.

Before going into some of the ways to develop, in all of our students, superior reading skills and musicianship, though, we need to touch on some of the practical questions for which answers are often sought. What about the older beginner who already reads books when he starts music study? Should he wait as long before starting to read music as the child starting at three? Probably not, for his desire to read tends to fade if he waits past age eight or nine. Postpone reading for as long as necessary to develop a musical memory, some imitative ability, and some musical instincts, but give him the satisfaction of reading in *limited amounts* if he is very eager to read. When his technical development is sound, he can go ahead with more intensive reading.

Another question bears on the effect a particular instrument has on the length of time necessary for the preparatory rote stage, and thus on the onset of the reading work. Pianists, who don't have to learn to hold their instruments, play in tune, and avoid scratching and squeaking, may have a shortened rote period in comparison with violinists. Since piano music is also more complex to learn by rote, because music for two hands is involved, there is another reason for beginning to read by the end of Suzuki Book I. To see chords along with a melodic line requires considerable reading practice, as does the job of responding to two clefs at once and fitting together two or more rhythms. To reach the point where sight-reading is not a tremendous labor, the pianist must spend more time, over-all, learning the reading craft. This is not to say that there should be an *emphasis* on sight-reading at about the second piano book level, for reading, at first, is mainly a supplementary aid to learning accurately the music which is being heard on records.

On this same question of how the type of instrument affects reading skills, a number of points need to be made regarding the problems presented by stringed instruments. All string players share the fact that while their music is not as difficult to read as that for piano, there are far more instrumental problems peculiar to strings which get in the way of *responding correctly to notation*. For one thing, students cannot see notes on the fingerboard. Thus they have difficulty learning to think note names when they place their fingers where the sound is produced. They tend to think finger numbers, or even just have a *feeling* that goes with a place on the staff or a sound in their minds, instead of associating an alphabet name with a note (except for the open-string notes). This is particularly true for traditionally trained students for two reasons: 1) having read music almost from the beginning, they have associated the place on the staff with a particular finger for a long time before beginning to shift (the Suzuki violinists often begin to read about the same time they begin to shift) and, 2) regular method books seldom show the 1st, 2nd or 3rd fingers over notes—only the 4th or O for open. As a result, those traditional students who have not progressed rapidly past the first position have trouble *noticing* the fingering, let alone *responding* to numbers they've seldom seen in their music, with fingers not trained to respond to directions—as when "Suzuki mothers" call out A-3, E-1, or some other location by string and finger.

String students also have a problem in playing with good rhythm at a steady tempo while following complex bowings. The better the bow arm skill and the more musical the rhythmic sense have become in that rote period before reading, the more likely it will be that rhythms will be read accurately and that tempo will be maintained in reading situations.

All of these factors must be considered while training a student to read. Too many teachers and parents who had piano work before that of an orchestral instrument have tried to apply exactly the same procedures in helping non-pianists read music. Much of the worry over reading may be caused by lack of clear analysis of differences between the reading content and needed responses for various instruments.

Still further questions concern neuro-muscular development and its importance in determining the time for reading work. If coordination is causing a student difficulty with technique, by all means postpone reading. Too often a student is simply beyond his depth of skill, working on pieces which are beyond him. Development of additional playing skills should come before advancing to reading of more difficult repertory. On the other hand, if the playing level is excellent but perceptual problems are a real concern, keep reading work confined to the conceptual stage, referred to later in this article, rather than bringing pressure for skilled and rapid reading.

Adjustment to each student's set of circumstances must be made, of course, but each teacher should develop a clear plan for the teaching of reading based on *principles which do not vary from one student to another*. The variable is the amount of time and repetition needed for each to reach a level of reading where he can function really well. The teacher's ingenuity must be applied to making each student eager and willing to work at reading.

Breaking Down the Learning Tasks in Reading

It is effective to classify the various symbols into different *codes* or *clue* systems. Use of such words is intriguing to many children, particularly boys. Teachers and parents should avoid the constant use of the term *reading,* especially with students having word-reading troubles. Most students enjoy the concept of music-reading as being a form of puzzle solving, especially if they are assured they can learn to do it well. They can also become Tune Detectives, or Private Eyes, in any of the following code categories:

PITCH: fingering, note patterns, intervals, letter names of notes, position on the staff, accidentals, keys, chords, and melodic lines.

TIME: tempo, duration of each note, accent pattern or meter, and rhythmic patterns.

FORM: phrasing, double bars (sections and endings), repeat marks, first and second endings, *D.C., Fine,* etc.

STYLE AND EXPRESSION: dynamics, expressive terms, articulation and textures, pedaling, bowing, etc.

The first two areas, pitch and time, are the most complex and difficult, and the tendency with most students and teachers is to pay exclusive attention to them when starting to learn a piece. The other codes are considered peripheral, to be added at a later date. This causes all sorts of trouble. As changes of weight, speed, or quality of motion are made after already learning the notes and rhythms well, both note accuracy and tempo will suffer. The later additions also tend to be forgotten quickly. How much better to learn a smaller amount of material each day, with attention to *all* of the coded markings! For this reason, it is good for students to learn to read the symbols for form and style early in the game, well ahead of the pitch and time factors. The student accomplishes it easily and becomes interested in reading. The codes he has learned will stand out on the page when he looks at it, and he will respond automatically to them while he goes on with the rational process of decoding notes and rhythms.

Another helpful classification is the division of reading development into three basic stages, following the language parallel.

FIRST STAGE: The pre-reading preparation during rote level learning when the student experiences musical and instrumental ideas which will be represented later by symbols. For those experiences, the teacher uses a vocabulary which prepares the student to respond automatically to the symbols and terms on the printed page when he is shown them.

SECOND STAGE: Introduction of the notational concepts for the experiences he has had. These may be shown in the music already learned or on charts, cards, or with other teaching aids. He should be expected to react physically, as he did earlier to verbal commands.

THIRD STAGE: The skill level, during which reading must be practiced regularly in order to gain accuracy in seeing and responding, within the limitations imposed by tempo and other pressures (like staying together with other players or keeping with a conductor).

The students may progress faster in some categories than in others. The teacher, keeping the categories and stages in mind, decides when a student is ready for the next stage of each category.

To use an appropriate metaphor, the first stage is the seed. In the second stage, the seed is planted. With sufficient nutriment and stimulation it sprouts in the third stage. Each code area has several seeds, of course, so a student may have one seed sprouting while another is being planted. If well trained, he may have become so familiar, let us say, with symbols for bowing and dynamics that he responds automatically with appropriate movements while concentrating on something else. Thus, we might say that he has passed through all three stages in the learning of bowing and dynamic codes, and those plants have flowered. At the same time, in the pitch area of reading, perhaps a seed is just sprouting and is being watered daily. Perhaps in rhythm reading, the seeds are being planted. Specific ideas will follow for the implementation of this process.

The First Stage

The first stage in learning to read is really part of the first stage of learning to play. The absence of "book learning" does not mean that students will have difficulty learning to read, since a fine teacher always teaches all early steps in relation to ultimate needs. He will try to lay a foundation for those needs, including music-reading. If certain essential experiences represented by symbols are developed during the first two or three years of playing, reading blocks do not occur later.

During the relatively long period of rote or direct learning, there are many ways in which to set the stage so that reading will be full of meaning for the student. Then he will not have to be told to look at the music when he falters, for he will be eager to search out directions on how to move, when to move, and where to put which fingers. He will understand the process, enjoy it, and be a successful reader. *At this preparatory stage, no visual aids are usually needed.*

A few children have difficulty in associating musical sounds with words like *up* and *down,* and *step* or *skip;* they have been able to straighten out their concepts by plotting out some music like Suzuki's "Perpetual Motion" or "Go Tell Aunt Rhody" on a graphic presentation of rising steps. This is still part of the preparatory First Stage since the stress is on ear-training and response.

Vocabulary and Musical Concepts

After compiling a list of vocabulary and symbols used in the first two or three books, the teacher should form a habit of using the terms whenever appropriate, whether while listening to music, watching others play, or working directly to learn a specific piece. Words can focus attention on the musical reality, and yet there are real sounds in today's newer forms of art music which are receiving new types of technical designations and which are not covered by our old vocabularies. It is very, very important not to let the ways we use our vocabularies limit a child's hearing and awareness of every aspect of pitch, timbre, and intensity. Playing by ear and experimenting to find sounds he likes limits growth less than playing from printed music, so we shoud be *wary of overdoing* the *vocabulary* at this stage.

If the student is under eight, there may be many verbal-musical associations to straighten out, as mentioned above. The use of high and low as opposed to *loud* and *soft* confuses young students. To them, *low* may mean *soft*. *Long* and *short* are confused with *slow* and *fast*. A string student has difficulty responding correctly to such words when they are called out by the teacher as he plays in a variety of tempos. He may need a long stroke, made rapidly in a slow tempo, or a short, slow stroke in a rapid tempo.

Foreign musical terms may be introduced after first using the English equivalent and obtaining a response, then adding the Italian term casually and synonymously. It is easy to do this with practically any term. One might speak of how "sweet" a particular tone is on a record and then go on to say, "it's such a BEAUTIFUL *dolce!*" After a certain amount of repetition of such a dual reference over a period of time, the term will cease being foreign and should evoke a musical response. If the teacher also praises the student for a sweet tone, as in, "I really like that *dolce* sound you made on the A," the physical response element will be strengthened and the student will remember how he made the *dolce*. Later, when he is introduced to the printed word, he will remember it easily and he will think *dolchay* and not *dolsee* when he sees it, for he will have heard it correctly pronounced before seeing the spelling.

Simple musical forms may be taught early through the ear and the themes given letter names each time they appear. It is helpful for memory training as well as interesting to the student. As an example of this, a seven-year-old-violinist was reviewing the first book before proceeding ahead. As he finished the "Happy Farmer" he exclaimed, "That's funny. I didn't know you could have an A A B A B A piece. I didn't notice it before. We've had A B A and A B B A and A B C A pieces but this one is still different." It was an intriguing discovery, and he'd had help on such thinking only in the first half of the book. It was obvious that he had not stopped thinking that way.

The important thing is to set a process in motion and use it consistently for a while. Along with reminding a student to "go back to the beginning!" one can add, "Da Capo!" The student is pleased when he can respond later without the English. Another important skill to foster is the recognition of the various *endings* as themes return only to lead off in a different direction. Special code colors for use in marking music might be introduced, with the student telling his mother which color to use for *form* in his music, as she marks with alphabet letters the phrase endings and thematic variations, while he looks on. When he listens to a record of the music, he may then like to follow along for the formal markings— gaining some perceptual training in the process.

To foster pride in knowledge of musical directions and response to them, a chart might be kept on which credit in some form is recorded for every good musical response to verbal (and later printed) terms. Special drives for terms within a specific category are more effective than using the full range of terms all the time.

To teach just "words" is obviously wrong. It is also poor teaching if it appears to the student to be testing for the sake of testing. Children quickly show disinterest if that is the case and parent and teacher need to revise the manner of presentation. Students should find the words useful in the context of their literature and not think they are isolated ideas.

To constantly refer to reading is another mistake. While much of a teacher's talk may be a forerunner of reading, it is best not to say so unless the student is begging to read and you wish to reassure him that you are preparing him for reading. Let reading be a natural response to language—first spoken, then printed—but not an unnecessary and boring detour from making music.

The most fun in reading comes with *rapid response* of the body's tools in turning a musical direction into a musical effect. It is also the most useful part of reading. The student who accomplishes that kind of response should be rewarded with recognition, both verbally from the teacher and parent, and from hearing his own improved skill. As Dr. Suzuki often says, "Children like what they can (do)."

Rhythm and Movement

Body response is obviously the natural way to approach intuitive understanding of tempo, rhythm patterns, and the mathematics of meter. The mind enters in later. Dalcroze, Kodaly, Orff and others have recognized this and developed specific systems which are reaching increasing numbers of children. Suzuki teachers do well to inform themselves of the practical applications and specific devices adaptable to instrumental teaching. All too often, children who have been introduced to music through one or the other of these approaches have not been helped to bridge the gap when they started to study an instrument. It isn't always an automatic transfer, so the parent and instrumental teacher must help start it.

What is the nature of a pre-school child's responses to rhythm besides rocking and swaying? For one thing, he feels a rhythm pattern as a whole better than he can keep track of the single notes making up the pattern—just as with words. When the pattern is repeated several times without pauses, many don't distinguish the repetition as such—it is one conglomerate. The first task in mastery, then, is simply learning how to keep track of units which are easily distinguishable. Asking a child to clap when a rhythm ends, or repeats, is one way which does not involve counting. Of course, nearly every three-year-old can say "one, two, three, etc.," but not all of them know what it means. When asked to play two tones, or two notes, or two bows, the child is more than likely to play four or five. Watch your language carefully, and teach him the meaning of what you consider to be a universally understood word: "two." Does the child also know the relationship between *two, second,* and *twice?*

Following a succession of printed notes may make it easy for older students, but the eyes of young children often jump around and do not act in an orderly way in searching for visual directions. To learn to count through the ears and through keeping track also of one's own movements is more helpful at this stage than depending upon printed music.

After mastering the task of consciously controlling just two repeated notes—then three or four—before stopping movement to *rest,* it is time to learn to count repetitions of the "Twinkle" basic rhythms. Tiny students enjoy playing a pattern on one note as many times as they are old. Before doing this successfully, they need to count the number of strokes and then patterns which the *teacher* plays for them.

From this step, they can learn to count the number of beats in one note. The mother or an advanced student should clap at a steady rate while the teacher plays three-beat notes, then two, then four. Start with one note and test the response. If good, proceed to playing a series of them for and with an audience which is clapping together by that time. One child might beat a drum while one or more students learn to say "quar-ter" with each beat. With such rhythmical sub-divisions, they will feel the beat more precisely and also learn its most common value name. They can learn next to say at half-speed, "h a l f--n o t e---" with a two beat note. Many teachers do not initiate such a counting method until the symbols are introduced, but it can be done very successfully with rote playing.

"Lightly Row" is an excellent piece to review when teaching children to count rhythmically, naming the note values: It goes,

"Quarter, quarter, h a l f---, n o t e---."

While possible to learn to sing the early songs this way when first learning to play them, it sidetracks attention to the techniques the teacher must teach. It is better, we think, to come back to this point when reviewing. "Twinkle, Twinkle" becomes,

"Quarter, quarter, quarter, quarter, quarter, quarter, h a l f-- n o t e---."

When played as in Variation I, it becomes,

"Ta-ka-ta-ka two eighths,"

or some of the many variants of ta-ka. An explanation is needed about the quicker sixteenths, pointing out their real name and showing that it is difficult to say it fast enough. Then move on to the "Allegro" and its combination of quarters, eighths and halves. The concept of fractions and relative durations is difficult in the usual mathematical manner for young children, but may be absorbed intuitively in music.

One of the nice things about using sixteenths from the beginning is that they become the smallest common unit felt, and lead to the process of *adding rather than the more difficult dividing.* A quarter note becomes the sum of four sixteenths rather than a fourth of a whole (whole notes are never used in the first violin book). The feeling of sixteenths becomes like graph paper on which the rhythm pattern is super-imposed like a design on a graph. Later when children see the printed music with its very "black" appearance, they accept it without the fear frequently associated with trying to play and read the faster denominations.

The dotted quarter may be taught in the "May Song," singing,

"Quarter-dot eighth quarter quarter,"

using a precise 3:1 ratio. Experience with dotted half notes is provided in the "Minuets" by Bach. Speak or sing them as,

"H a l f---n o t e---dot---."

Meter is best understood by keeping track of the number of beats between regular principal accents, rather than the number between two visible bar lines. Conducting and counting together are preferable to counting only.

Teach the student how to conduct the basic 2/4, 3/4 and

4/4 meters. Two-beat rhythms of down and up beats are the natural starting point, and should be associated with the *strong-weak effect* pieces in either 2/4 or cut-time which abound in the first book. The "Minuets," of course, provide practice in counting the 3/4 meter, and secondary accents in 4/4 time may be demonstrated in "Long, Long Ago." The important trick in helping each child to know what he is doing, rather than just waving his arms in response to a generalized feeling, is to thoroughly master the conducting pattern in one piece of each meter without pressuring for quantity of work in this line. It is an activity to which a teacher may switch when children seem tired, for it is a change of pace away from the instrument, and most probably the child is tired mentally and will revive with a different task. It is an effective device in group sessions, too, with different students taking turns conducting the same piece.

An allied activity helps teach awareness of fluctuation of tempo as in the *ritardando* and *fermata* of Dr. Suzuki's "Allegro." Taste and judgment are important in tempo fluctuations and there is a good way to develop it, in addition to the hearing of lots of good music well-played. Have one student act as conductor while others play. He may hold the music back any place he chooses and to any degree. Those playing or listening may approve, criticize and discuss. There is sure to be laughter frequently. Musical taste becomes a matter of pride when the children can be praised for good judgment in such a game. The young conductor should try to do this sometimes with good taste and some times with exaggerated poor taste to test the audience. What child won't notice the awkwardness of poorly placed and timed alterations in tempo after having heard good performances. Children glow with enjoyment of this type of musical humor. Repetition with variety keeps them alert.

Tempo games or activities are enjoyed most after students have learned the pieces with tempo names. It was thoughtful of Dr. Suzuki to provide some of his compositions with tempo terms for names, for it serves to call attention rather early to such words. We notice that children who have played the "Allegro" and "Allegretto" pick the words right up when heard in a new connection. Later their eyes gravitate to the words in new music. We don't hear children saying that they forget what *Allegro* means. It is perfect proof that the experience preceding the symbol aids reading, at least *if* the child has been made conscious of his experience. The intuitive experience needs to be appreciated and recognized in order to become fully useful as a foundation for rational thinking in artistic matters.

A tempo game usually enjoyed is to have one child play one of the simple pieces at any tempo he chooses while the other students call out the tempo they think he is using. Or at a lesson the teacher plays while the student responds. At first, use a choice of only two tempos. Children are ecstatic when the extremes of *vivace* and *largo* are added to the more moderate terms. Marching to "Twinkle," played to the spoken tempo commands of a student or teacher, is another good device (and one which may be played to the command of a large hand-printed tempo card in the second stage). Just walking tempos at lessons before playing them is another good device, even with the most advanced students. *Andante,* naturally, is a very good starting point, stressing its implicit meaning— walking.

Expression, Style, Articulation and Movement

Many advanced students, who have been trained to see and understand terms, do not actually produce the appropriate sounds when playing from the printed page. If we wish our Suzuki youngsters to be any different as they mature, we must stimulate them to move physically in response to what they hear mentally or see on paper, and again the time to start is in the pre-reading stages. Specific instrumental techniques must be taught, of course, and a child helped to understand that there are ways to use fingers and arms to achieve each of the effects represented by words and symbols. Imitation is fine—and the only way to learn shadings and nuance—but it must be very conscious before reading is begun.

Each teacher expects to accomplish this but is easily discouraged and thwarted by the awkwardness of most students. Perhaps we don't remember our own awkwardness, and then seeing literally thousands of Japanese children moving most responsively and skillfully as they play has convinced thousands of Western teachers and parents that Western children have inherently poorer coordination. Let us not succumb to that defeatist idea. Those of us who have been able to watch beginning students in Japan have seen the care and patience which it takes for teachers and parents to turn typical three-year-olds into skillful performers of the "Twinkle" variations over a period of a year or so.

Their feedback sense, enabling them to know when they have done the right thing, is developed through questioning, "Was that a good tone? Did you like it? Can you do it again? Did you stop your bow without a crunch? Is your thumb still bent?" So run the questions, and when the student can no longer concentrate he is let off the hook and the lesson ends. This has been told many times, but it needs saying on this subject of reading and responding.

This is *our* job as teachers, and it may include suggesting to parents that they need to find additional activities outside of music to engage the child's mind in purposeful mastery of his head and shoulder muscles, his arms and fingers—in fact, of the whole neuro-muscular system—so that printed directions will have power over his body. When a child comes to us at the age of three or four, it is often the first situation where he is expected to do anything with precision, and we must initiate with patience and gentleness the maturation process so he can. Of course, we don't mean that he should do other things just so he can play the piano or the violin or cello a little better, but we hope he will become a superior human being by developing well his body tools to serve his mind and spirit.

171

SUZUKI CONCEPT

Some of our young students are enjoying the finger activities found in a charming book reprinted from the turn of the century. It offers a greater variety of motions than most modern nursery school books and opens up the world of the farm to city youngsters. It is *Finger Plays for Nursery and Kindergarten* by Emilie Poulsson (Dover).

What is wrong with American children learning to eat with chopsticks? It's a handy ability in this world of international eating. By comparison with spoon holding, chopsticks probably give Japanese children a headstart on manipulative finger skills. Origami (paper folding), which becomes part of a young child's life in Japan, develops dexterity, precision, and memory. When we encourage this skill to get started around two to three, while the child is most imitative and is interested in processes more than in results, we will find that he does become amazingly skilled, provided he is allowed to repeat and repeat a few operations rather than rushing on to fold a new kind of creature. Just a few simple figures for a long time is best. To fold 1,000 cranes is a custom which brings luck in Japan—perhaps for a good reason. What practice one would gain! We must make it lucky for a child to practice a difficult spot 1,000 times.

In music, not only *difficult spots must be repeated* and repeated. There need to be pieces in which important skills are featured, and those *pieces must be used over a long period of time.* Dr. Suzuki features "Twinkle," his "Allegro," the second "Minuet" by Bach, the Handel "Bourrée," the "Two Grenadiers," the Bach "Bourrée" and the Vivaldi "Concerto in A Minor" in that way. Others are important, too, but for really solid accomplishment, a young player will need certain pieces to be featured over others for purposes of long term repetition. In Dr. Suzuki's book of *reading* exercises, he requires the same kind of repetitive work at ever increasing speed of response.

If all of the dynamics and other expressive factors, the stylistic textures of touch, and articulation of phrasing are built into these featured pieces and repeated enough, the accompanying techniques will be applied instinctively to other appropriate music. One of the goals is recognition of these experiences when reading unfamiliar music in a familiar period or style.

The best teaching devices are those which are both stimulating and economical in terms of maximum results with minimum material. Besides the repetition of repertory, as opposed to a large repertory played superficially, there are built-in challenges in the use of well-known children's games adapted to our needs. *Simon Says* is unlimited. "Simon Says touch the scroll. Simon Says pluck the E string. Touch the bridge. Simon Says put the bow on the A string without a sound." It's an activity in which even three-year-olds find pleasure, although they usually cannot understand being "caught." No matter. The big point, besides speedy reactions, is that children who don't want to repeat week after week certain important learning steps are willing to do it when "Simon says" to do it. They become alert, responsive, and gain steadily in the abilities to move their eyes, hands, and arms around.

"Playing Statue" is another such game—one good for making students aware of the positions of their wrists, fingers, elbows, or any other part of the anatomy the teacher is working on. "Freeze" may find them in a good or bad position, but at least they can discover which. The signal for "freezing" may be the stopping of the accompaniment, which is also a good device for sensitizing. Students at a lesson might be asked to stop *themselves* at the end of every phrase—to check an arm height or the position of the bow on the string. They might have as a goal the recognition of *dominant* chords. In that case, the teacher might clap on a few of the dominant chords at first and then leave the rest up to the student to recognize and stop on. The stops might also be made before certain notes that are always missed by students.

"Treasure Hunt" is a magic name to students. One may search for tonal treasures for a week or for the duration of a lesson. Or the treasure might be punctuation points in the music, unusual harmonic color, modulations, or, when listening to students playing solos, it might be ways in which each soloist had improved. Later on in the next stage, when notation has been introduced, the search might be for such points found in the printed music. A teacher might prepare ahead of time for a treasure hunt by preparing clues on slips of paper: find three *crescendos* on the first page, find two *ritardandos* on the second, and two *signature* changes on the third.

Games involving speedy response to the specialized roles of the two hands (and pedal foot) are active and valuable. The student should raise the correct arm quickly—the arm which bears the principal responsibility at the moment as the teacher plays a piece being worked on and pauses at places important for one or the other hand: a rhythm, a tone color, a line of melody, an important chord, a switch from *legato* to *staccato.*

String students may be trained to be more analytical of difficulties in this manner, since they have a different type of specialization. *While the right hand selects the pitch, the left hand produces the tone of the same note.* The right is responsible for the rhythm *except* during slurs. Articulation and emphasis are mostly in the right hand, but during slurred runs the left hand percussive action becomes important. The dynamics are obviously in control of the right arm, but the quality of tone and timbre are at one moment the job of the bow arm and in the next of the vibrating left hand. A group game which is fun only if done rapidly enough, and which is great for the ages over seven or eight, consists of having two teams. Each team takes turns calling out an expressive term or a technical term such as a special style, and the opposite team gets a point only if every member raises the arm responsible. Or, one student on each team is chosen as the leader who will play any of the well-known tough spots in the repertory to which the other team must respond with the hand most responsible. String students soon discover how much of the time the right arm is raised and are helped to get over the idea that the mind should be on fingering all the time.

Bow direction and arm movement control are areas which require a great deal of work, since these seem weak in America, at least. No matter by what methods students have been taught, bowing precision is sadly lacking in most high school orchestras, and college conductors even complain about their performance majors' carelessness in this regard. All teachers have felt it significant, too, that students can look at their bows, slipping toward the fingerboard, without making any attempt to correct the sound point. They have puzzled over the many students who insist they just took a down-bow even though they may have for the fifth consecutive time taken an up-bow. Is it a lack of caring, of sensing the importance of this aspect of playing? Is it the lack of careful guidance in specifics from a parent in the early years of study? Is it a lack of correct analysis of the bowing problems on the part of the teacher? It is probably a combination of all three, but whatever the cause, things may be improved by certain important forms of stimulation during the warm-up period in practice, lessons, and group work. Without plenty of work, it will be fruitless to expect students to correctly respond to bowing marks while reading.

The bow-tip-control exercises of Dr. Suzuki work wonders in the directional sense. The deep-knee-bends on the strong beats of pieces, done while playing or listening to records, accomplish the sense of down and up also. Working on bow follow-through by letting the arm carry the bow across the strings at the end of an important full length up-bow until the hand can touch the violin body on the far side is another. Doing the deep bends during the rests in the Gossec "Gavotte" helps students learn to make down-bow "recoveries." All falling or dropping motions lead to a sense of gravity as a reference point and heighten the awareness of direction. Piano students, too, must develop this sense for the control of shoulder, elbow, wrist, and hand movements, angles, and working heights. The lateral motions are important for both strings and piano, but are not as basic to tone as are the vertical directions.

To help a string student master slurring and the linking of detached notes, mothers can learn to pantomime the bowing with the teacher's help. The student then "reads" her gestures. Students who work this way in the first three books learn to read bow directions easily. A six-year-old boy, having worked his way through the second "Minuet" in this manner, asked how his mother knew when to slur. She showed him how it looked, and suggested that he mark over the slurs with a red pencil. Together, they then listened to the record and followed through the music for the segment to be learned that day. She guided his hand along at first, until his eyes became accustomed to the rate of reading in each part. They discussed the sounds of the smooth slurs as contrasted with the detached but linked slurs. Then they practiced enough times, while she pantomimed the bowing again, until he could remember the feel without looking at her motions. This mother used common sense and combined the first and second reading stages almost immediately on this slurring factor, the notational concept being very easy. They continued this sequence of practice steps through the first three books, but gradually discontinued the red pencil. Needless to say, the boy's bow directions were always flawless. At the same time, his eyes received perceptual training without actually playing from music.

From beginning to end of work on a piece, the emotional and musical feeling response to the piece should be the foundation upon which the ability to play musically must be built. Strong physical activity during some of the record listening is advisable. Dancing to the repertory is stimulating to some, and conducting is wonderful. Pairing contrasting styles in the music with contrasting styles of dancing or marching is another approach. Smooth-rough, strong-weak, bold-gracious, growing louder-getting softer—these are natural contrasts which appear commonly in music, of course, as *legato-staccato, forte-piano, marcato-grazioso,* and *crescendo-diminuendo.* Later, reading these terms evokes an interested response.

Fingering and Pitch Names

For children taught traditionally to read from the beginning of study, the usual custom has been, of course, to teach the names of the notes right away. While it might seem essential in learning music that students should learn the names of the notes without delay, the problem encountered in working with very young children is that the child must learn to control his fingering from the first, also, and he has difficulty concentrating on more than one thing at a time. Also, *fingers just don't have letter names.* It is true that a student must find certain keys on the piano, or certain exact places on one of the four strings of a violin or cello, but much of the common inaccurate fingering which develops later may be avoided if the teacher first develops accuracy of response as he calls out a finger number. The key or the place on the string may be demonstrated but not given a name until a little later, depending upon the individual case. It is something of a surprise at first to watch this being done in Japan, but it will not harm later development of pitch association if the teacher plans natural steps to proceed along, and doesn't *delay too long* in making use of the letters. String students do learn the four open string letters as points of reference, and piano students will learn at least the C and G anchor points for "Twinkle."

Some piano courses have been designed to speed reading by teaching the association of a key on the piano with a line on the staff before stressing pitch names, since to name a line and then think a finger is less direct and requires an intermediate translation step. With string players, this has always happened to some extent except for the relatively small number who possess pitch recognition ability before even beginning to study the instrument. The teacher may work hard on pitch naming, but the student is still quicker to associate the feel of a specific finger with a place on the staff.

The members of one of the most famous string quartets were discussing with us the idea of rote training, and they began to exchange data on just when each had started to actually think notes by name while playing. They discovered that each had not developed this ability until around the age of 16 when playing advanced orchestral and chamber music which was harmonically complex and could not be played in any other manner than by knowing exactly the flat, sharp, or natural aspect of each note. And yet, they had received solid conservatory training in one of Europe's leading music schools.

Because the young students we are now teaching have not developed the necessary nerve pathways which permit them to put a second finger down without looking at it, we must do considerable work on this ability for a few months. Use both ordinal and cardinal numbers to teach the name of each finger. The first and last fingers do not cause confusion, but the inside ones need a good deal of work. Make games of moving a specific finger. Have children shake their hands and then hold up the finger called for. Have them do it "blind," putting their hands behind their backs. Then have the mothers do the same thing while the students call out the fingers and look for their mothers' mistakes.

When the child has learned several pieces, and begins to drop some from the daily routine, he reaches the stage of being carefree and careless. He becomes cocky, since he has also learned the logic of the fingerboard, soundwise, or of the keyboard. He begins to make fingering mistakes. The problem for piano students of the reversal of numbering directions in the two hands poses problems, too. (When the piano student puts one hand on top of the other, he is pleased to discover that the third fingers are together, even though the fifth is over the first, and the fourth is over the second.) The violin student, about this time, becomes impatient to connect notes without pausing and finds he can fish around to locate a note.

When he makes fingering mistakes, it is better not to say, "That's wrong fingering." Try instead, "Your second finger didn't answer the phone. Are you sure you called the right number? Perhaps no one was at home." Children enjoy knowing that they have a communication system in their bodies and that this nervous system may be compared with the telephone. Wrong numbers, new numbers, disconnected numbers, phones off the hook—they help to put over the idea painlessly to a school-age child. Better still, the game encourages concentration.

When the job of developing finger response to numbers has been achieved, it is time to consider letter naming. The time for this varies tremendously with different students. The student, if a pianist, has learned to associate his fingers and piano keys with the sounds and parts of a specific piece. Patterns are a great aid, for the student learns the fingering groupings which lie together following certain anchor notes. These may be the first notes to have their letter names stressed. The C's usually are the first of the anchor notes, with the skip to G in "Twinkle" providing another anchor position. Since many pre-school children (and some older ones) do not know the alphabet in order, even though they can name all of the letters, they cannot automatically understand how to name the series of notes up and down the scale. To help them, take small scale sections at first, and learn the notes backwards and forwards. BAG and GAB provide fun for those learning to spell. Doing it in both hands, all over the piano, gives practice in the reverse fingering of the two hands.

Patterns up and down from the open strings are just as important for the string students. The very young students soon learn to associate a sound with a place on the fingerboard. They often develop a type of absolute pitch dependent upon fingering rather than letter names. When they hear the teacher play any of the notes in the one octave A major scale used for the early pieces, most students can imitate them accurately without having to look at the teacher's fingering and without hesitating.

179

A good way for violin students to start the transfer to letter name associations is to talk about the ABC's in connection with the "Perpetual Motion" after it has been thoroughly learned. Explain that each finger represents a family of notes called by a letter name, and that there are low, middle and high members of each family: *A Flat,* or low; *A Natural,* or middle; and *A Sharp,* or high. Go to the piano, if possible, to clarify this with the white and black notes, having the student play the *white* ABC's and compare the sound of the first three notes of the "Perpetual Motion" to discover that he must sharp the C.

Start singing the first four-note pattern of the "Perpetual Motion" slowly by letter names, then repeat at a faster tempo. Comment on the difficulty of saying C# rapidly, twice. Decide together whether to sing the whole song saying the letters only, or adding the sharps (which would be essential for the piano student). The more discussion and experimentation, the more likely that the student will be able to remember the sharps even if he doesn't say them *every* time. Then have the student *discover* the names of the notes on the following sequences, using logic. Make it a daily assignment to sing the first phrase of this piece by letter name—in strict but moderate tempo—for at least a month to develop tongue habits:

"ABC#C#, BC#DD, C#DEC#, DBEE,"

After a week or so, add the second pattern of the piece and have it likewise as part of the daily assignment. The tongue needs to learn to "think" the alphabet backwards. If the student is not saying the names of the sharps in singing the notes, remind him occasionally of the names of the notes that he plays.

Correlating the positions of the notes on the fingerboard with the piano keyboard has always been difficult, even for adult beginners on the stringed instruments because of the *diminished fifths.* To do so requires both musical sense and reasoning ability. It is certainly more natural for children to absorb music intuitively and later figure out why they must place a finger in a high position on one string and a low position on the next string in order to play the fifth from B to F.

In teaching alphabetical patterns, we should apply Suzuki's principles of economical uses of some basic literature and be very repetitive in just one piece, or part of it, to put over those concepts. Select scale type pieces with few skips and with melodic lines both up and down—and then keep working on the same pieces over a long period, even as the students advance through the repertory.

In the Suzuki repertory, pieces which are well-suited to the purpose are "Long, Long Ago," "Go Tell Aunt Rhody," "Allegro," and the "Allegretto." The piece chosen should not be so long that the child tires and becomes confused while naming the notes by letters as he plays or listens.

An ear-training supplement to the scale line naming in the pieces is a game of keeping track of notes that the teacher plays up and down the scale line, turning around at any point as he pleases. First he gives the name of the starting note, and after that each student *silently* thinks the note letter of each note until the teacher stops, whereupon the students call out what they think the note was. The tempo should be slow, but steady. The note progression may be patterned or may wander. The child enjoys *thinking* the notes silently as the teacher plays.

As students gain accuracy in keeping track of the letters, the examples may gradually be lengthened from five or six notes to a dozen or more. After much success in the simpler step-wise work, introduce skips of a third.

The students later will enjoy the inclusion of an occasional accidental which naturally stands out strikingly. To develop awareness of half and whole steps by ear, teach them to follow the chromatic scale. But first let them play it on the piano, naming each note, with black keys named as sharps when ascending and flats when descending. It may be possible with some students to challenge them to name the notes of a whole-tone scale by ear, and to be able to follow along in the same game-type procedure as described above.

In this First Stage, and again in the Second Stage when the ideas for notating musical experiences are presented, it is most important to move along by such easy and natural steps that the students cannot fail. They must have *solid* steps from which they may be propelled to the next concept or skill, though. They should be lead to an increased understanding of musical logic through understanding musical notation, whether verbal or written, and should make notation an aid to musical playing.

The Second Stage—Pointers and Observations

The pointers which follow will not all apply to every age. Some are for the youngest students, other observations are principally for parents or teachers, and some are equally valid for all.

Teaching through discovery is of maximum importance in music-reading work. Give some historical background, brief but enough to stir some excitement over Man's long quest for ways to notate musical sounds and effects. The student is motivated to take advantage of what has been developed in notation. He should try to imagine that he has never seen any music. He may work out ways for himself to indicate any of the categories of musical experience in which he is especially interested. One nine-year-old boy, who had played violin entirely without music since beginning two years earlier, was so excited about learning to read that at his first reading lesson there was a barrage of questions whose answers he never forgot: "How do they show loud and soft? How do quarter notes look? And half-notes? How are slurs shown? How do they tell you to slow down?"

The games and teaching devices suggested for the First Stage can often be transformed from verbal directions to written ones by showing the corresponding symbol or words on large cards. Two sizes of card may be made, one for group work and one for individual work.

- Looking at music while listening to a recording of it is an important way to help develop associations. Certainly mothers should do this.

- We shouldn't "throw the book" at the student at once, but should concentrate on one phase of reading at a time and use it intensively.

- At this stage, all cards should be shown long enough to be studied by the student, and then at later stages flashed with increasing speed. Speed drills are especially required in the Third Stage.

- In the Second Stage the teacher should seek quick reactions to the symbols on cards or in a music book. In the Third Stage the students should be expected to be able to read well at a steady musical tempo instead of playing haltingly at a slow tempo.

- Concepts should be set by demonstration more than talk. Help from an advanced student at group lessons is beneficial. He may demonstrate how to play steadily while the teacher holds up the direction cards, or he may show the cards while the teacher helps the students to move quickly.

- Body response to the various codes can be separated effectively from the actual instrumental playing. The floor staff is an excellent way to do this in pitch reading. The ideas and teaching aids produced by Madeline Carabo-Cone should be investigated for this purpose. Those who already know the materials and ideas of Dalcroze, Orff, or Kodaly in this area of experience will see many ways to incorporate them into the reading experience of Suzuki method students.

- At this point, mistakes in rhythm, time, or tempo should be corrected not as much by counting as through careful use of records. Many students who learn a piece by reading will play wrong time very rhythmically, and others will play correct time values without sounding rhythmical, failing to project a sense of the beat. "Ask the record what you are doing wrong in the third line," a teacher may say. Or, "Ask the record what you have overlooked about the tempo." After the student has corrected a passage in that way by himself, he should play the passage while looking at the music to find which note values or tempo marks were previously missed.

• Finding accents in music needs explanation. Some will be shown in the customary form or as a small inverted *V* or as a *sforzando*. The regular accent scheme, customarily associated with each meter, however, must be understood. Bar lines should be explained as being placed perceding the principal regular accents. That is what meter is all about. Secondary accents in *Common* time and in compound meters should be explained, too.

• If parents have been singers, wind players, or pianists before their children began studying a string instrument, the parents should be given a clear understanding of the use of slurs— those curved lines which immediately appear to them to be phrasing marks requiring *legato*. While the majority of slurs are *legato* in string music also, they are usually only small parts of phrases and frequently only indicate the bow direction as being the same for a series of detached or semi-detached notes. Seldom are there phrasing marks in string music, although an occasional breath mark or parallel diagonal lines will indicate a break.

• The contour relationships on the staff—the line of the music and the intervals between the notes—are more important to vocalists than are the specific note names. Instrumentalists, on the other hand, must be more specific.

• Special interests of a student, or even special difficulties, are factors which sometimes determine when he is first introduced to a printed symbol. At the same time he may be given limited reading in the repertory for that particular symbolic guide. Beware of trying to cure a weak harmonic sense or pitch sense by note reading. Those weaknesses reveal a need for more ear-training, not more eye-training.

• Composing and writing down music specifically for a certain child—often while he watches—can be an effective treatment of his problems. By using the first rhythm variation of "Twinkle," while changing note patterns, dynamics, bow groupings, and textures, it is possible to diagnose and remedy the element of notation he does not understand.

• Teach the position of notes on the staff only after the student has been prepared to understand clefs, as described in the next section. For complete understanding of the advantages of clefs—of having more than one line, for instance—use a one line staff first, calling it in turn by any note name desired.

• Ask students to discover what *two* elements of music are indicated by each note (pitch and meter). Develop this point thoroughly and maintain their interest in both pitch and duration factors so that they will never ignore either one.

• There are many methods of notating fingering before introducing regular notes. A good one for strings, because it also trains the eye in the left to right and up and down motions, would look like this for "Twinkle." (The bars are for placekeeping more than for meter.)

```
E _____ 0 0 | 1 1 0 − |           |
A   0 0          |         | 3 3 2 2 | 1 1 0 −
```

• Reading more advanced music for skill at a steady tempo comes in the Third Stage, but the student is prepared for it in the Second Stage. Using very easy music, the student is given the concept of correlating all the categories of symbols in order to play them correctly at a steady tempo.

• In piano work, call attention to the treble and bass clefs and to the fact that the left-hand frequently changes from bass to treble clef.

• Teaching aids may be made by the teacher very easily, taking advantage of the various quick printing or instant reproduction processes. A generous supply of various sized *blank* staves is a must. They should be filled in with a felt-tip pen in front of the student, or used by the student himself, or prepared in advance with examples of different notational concepts. Thin, inexpensive paper may be used for the one-shot uses, and index weight stock used for permanent or repeated uses. Plan the spacing to permit one or two staves to fit the standard or legal sizes of paper.

• Other useful teaching resources include: 1) chalkboard and/or large pieces of paper for drawing while listening to music; 2) a pair of note-finders of the magnetic type, one for the teacher and one for the student to copy what the teacher shows. (String teachers may prefer to make their own using just a single clef with lines spaced to fit the available note magnets and with a metal backing to which the magnets will stick.); 3) some orchestral scores of works popular with children or of concertos they hear most often; 4) some baroque works, which have less complicated scores; 5) some music for other instruments: winds, piano, organ, percussion, strings, guitar, for comparison; 6) some examples of *avant garde* notation; 7) examples of medieval notation, such as that found on some gift-wrapping paper.

• Teaching aids may be divided into several categories:
  —those used to put over a concept
  —those used for games or puzzles
  —those for the student to use at home.

• In making visual aids teachers should experiment with such ideas as different sizes and proportions of notes or spacing, to find the best ones for effortless reading by the student. The teacher should keep in mind the age of the student and the distance from which the aids are to be read (on a music stand, before a large group, in a small room or a large room, for example).

• Many kinds of flash cards are available in music stores. They are nearly all geared to the piano, with two clefs and nothing below middle C in the treble clef. Violinists need practice in the notes from G up to C below the treble clef. Cards with musical terms and dynamics are good for any instrument.

• Test the focal distance of a young reader by moving a bright, attractive object on a rod back and forth about 18 inches from the child's eyes. Watch his eyes track. Gradually bring it closer, still moving it from side to side. If his eyes no longer track at a certain distance, you know he is not seeing the object. Be sure, then, that flash cards and other reading devices are shown to the child at the proper distance. (Remember this fact with young violinists, who sometimes cannot even *see* their bows on the string.)

• Perceptual training in seeing from left to right and up and down may be aided by some experiences outside of music. The "Peanuts" cartoon strips, for example, have very simple pictures with little change from one frame to the next. Reading them, the child will use his eyes much as he should do in music, scanning up and down and then moving on, only looking back occasionally to compare for slight variations in meaning. This resembles looking back in music to verify a key signature or checking an accidental used earlier in the same measure.

• Along with introducing new concepts, be sure to review (in game form if possible) concepts learned previously.

Games and Devices

If students beginning to read will do as Dr. Suzuki suggests and go back to Book I, already learned by rote, they will discover how black the notation is for sixteenth notes in the "Twinkle Variations" but how easy they are in actual playing. This will help to alleviate any future fear of similar notation.

• Cards may be prepared which have fingering patterns: 1–3–4, 1–3–1, 1–2–3, etc. Students should hold their hands over their heads or behind their backs while moving their fingers in these patterns, to develop the feeling of directing the fingers from within, "playing from the inside, out."

• *Flash cards.* Cards with signs for repeat, *D.C., Fine,* or Double bar, may be flashed to students as they are playing to direct what to do next.

• *"Private Eyes."* Have students become detectives or "Private Eyes," searching through music for measures that "look alike."

Also search for measures that are almost alike, and point out the differences. "How many are there of each kind?"

- *Matching cards.* Make ten pairs of matching cards, each with three or four notes. Shuffle them and have the student try to match up the pairs.

Make sets of cards for each interval. Also include some misfits that are close but not exactly alike.

- *Where did the music stop?* While a record is playing or the teacher is playing, the student follows the music, pushing along a small disc. When the music stops he leaves his disc on the last note for the teacher to see. This game may also be played in groups.

- *Treasure hunt.* The teacher may say, "There are six F's in the first line. Can you find them?" "How many sharps are there in the second line?" "Can you locate seven *crescendos* on the first page?" "Find twenty-five slurs in the 'Second Minuet.'"

- *Intervals.* Choose examples of thirds, fourths, fifths, octaves, etc., from the first five or ten pieces. (The broken thirds at the beginning of "Lightly Row," the fifth in "Song of the Wind," the thirds in "Children's Song," the arpeggio with a fourth that opens the "May Song," the descending scale patterns in "Twinkle" and "Long, Long Ago.") Make large cards which quote a measure or two including these intervals, but do not indicate the particular spots. Let the children play from the cards and guess which piece they are taken from.

- Have a group of students look through printed music for some particular interval and see who can find the most examples.

- *Volley Ball Games.* Students are divided into two teams. A piece is started by one team and passed over to the other team at a given signal, such as a clap from the teacher. Other varieties may be worked out. One team may play all the *forte* passages, the other all the *piano* passages; one may do all the *legatos,* the other all the *staccatos;* one team play first appearance of a melody or a motive, the other its repetition. With pianists at two pianos, one may play all the tonic chords in the left hand, the other all the dominants and subdominants. The ball may also be passed from one team to the other at every bar line.

• *Command Performance.* While the students are playing a well-known piece, the teacher or another student may hold up a card with some kind of command, such as a dynamic mark, a *legato* or *staccato* sign, a tempo indication, or a bowing mark. The students continue playing but try to follow the commands on the cards.

• While children march or move to music, have them use their feet to make the dynamics indicated on large cards displayed by the teacher, or at home by the mother.

• *Reverse Commands.* Play all *legato* notes in a piece *staccato,* and all *staccatos, legato;* play all dynamics reversed, using *mezzo-forte* as the midpoint; play the bowing in reverse; ignore all the slurs; accent every third finger; play every "B" softly; make a *crescendo* on every scale section.

• *One Concept Missing.* Copy a section of a piece on a large card. On each card, leave out *only one* concept, such as clef, rhythm, pitch of notes, dynamics, bar lines, meter signature, fingering, *legato* or *staccato* signs, tempo sign. Have the students study the cards and compare with the original to see if they can discover what is missing. Have them use musical terminology to explain what is missing.

• *Concentration.* We saw this game played by pre-schoolers at the nursery school in the Suzuki Institute in Matsumoto, Japan. The children were learning to recognize *kanji,* the difficult Chinese characters used in writing Japanese. The teacher read a favorite story aloud. When she came to a word represented by one of the *kanji* on large cards the student who could first pick out the right card was given that card to hold. This went on until all the cards were distributed. After that, whenever that word was used, the student holding the appropriate card would raise it up for the group to see. When the story was finished, the cards were turned face-down on their desks. The teacher would call out a word and the students were given turns to try to locate the right card. When it was found it would be proudly brought up to the front and put on display. Each child had just one try and then the turn went on to the next. When the cards were finally all back on display the children named them as the teacher pointed. It was a stimulating game that all the children seemed to enjoy.

To adapt this game to music-reading, one might select dynamics or expressive word terms, or rhythmic figures which recur in the piece to be played. The teacher plays or has a record played. When the child hears his effect he raises his card.

• *Single Note Recognition.* Almost any child can succeed in locating a single note, having been shown a picture of it first. He may sing or play it each time it appears with the teacher playing all the other notes. A different note may be featured each week.

The group plays a simple piece with each student assigned one note to play whenever it occurs. Then the piece is repeated with each student given a different assigned note. The teacher or another student may be the director to point to the right person for each note as it occurs, or it may be done without a director. The playing may be unfamiliar music read from the music, or a familiar piece played by memory.

• *Spelling Bees.* The teacher dictates letters by their position on the fingerboard (or keyboard). For instance, for strings, E, open; E, second finger; E, second. The student tries to figure out the word. For piano give the student a certain position at the keyboard, such as thumb on C, and dictate the finger numbers. Have students guess the word played on the piano by fingers 3,5,5 (egg). For strings, at first try all words possible with only open strings (ad, add, deed, dad, etc.). Later, combine open strings with fingered notes. Later have repeated letters played in different places on the fingerboard. For piano, challenge the students to play the same word in as many ways as possible on the keyboard. At first they may just shift octaves on the whole word. Later point out that each letter may be shifted to make a new keyboard pattern. Challenge them to find how many ways they can play *cafe, bag, dead,* etc.

Floor Staff. (the distance between lines should allow for a child's foot to fit into the spaces easily.)

1) The teacher plays a single note and all the students stand on the proper line or space.

2) The teacher plays a series of notes and each child, in turn, stands on the right line or space for his note in the melody.

3) The teacher places students in the order of one of the pieces they all know. Students try to identify the piece.

4) The teacher names a location on fingerboard or keyboard and students stand in the proper place.

5) The variation *Simon Says* may add spice to the dictation. "*Simon Says* stand on the D line." (Do it.) "Stand on the A line." (Don't do it, because *Simon* didn't say so.)

• *Note Concentration.* Violin students may concentrate on reading and fingering the notes while the teacher draws the bow for them. This is especially good for students who have difficulty in coordination.

• *One-line Staff.* To help students understand note-relations on a staff, begin with a single line. Let each child have a card with a single line and three counters like round note heads. First the teacher asks them to turn the card over to the blank back side and arrange their three counters in the order of high, middle and low notes. Then they turn the card over and do the same thing, with the teacher pointing out that the line might make it easier to tell how far apart the notes are. Some children will catch on immediately, but if there are four children there may be four quite distinct ways of arranging the notes. Perhaps one child will put the high and low notes just above and below the single line. The teacher can point out that it is easier to tell how far notes are above or below if they are close to the line. For notes farther up or down perhaps we need another line. Thus the staff is explained as a kind of ruler to measure how far up and down we want to go.

There are several ways in which a single line staff may be used:

1) Have children copy pattern demonstrated by teacher. It is surprising how difficult it may be for children to see the pattern of high and low and duplicate it.

2) Children place the three notes in a row *on the line.* The teacher plays the same note three times on an instrument. Then he plays again, changing one note. He sees if the students can make the corresponding change in their pattern. First he may change the third note, making it lower. Next he may change the third note, making it higher. The next time, he changes the second note, and finally the first note.

3) Assign a letter name to the single line. Then ask the children to name the notes above and below. Repeat the pattern game of (2) but this time have them name the notes. Now change the assigned letter name of the single line and continue the same game. It may be changed several times during the course of the game, so that the students understand that it is the relationship of one note to the next that is important.

4) Additional counters may be given each student so that longer patterns are possible.

5) A second line is added to the staff, so that a wider range of notes may be used. With two lines there is now a range of five notes.

6) Five lines may be used next. Then the teacher points out that on the violin one needs places for about four octaves of notes, and on the piano for seven and a half octaves. The students should figure out ways of accommodating so many notes. Many varieties of solution may be offered. Having a large number of identical lines soon becomes obviously impractical. Someone may suggest graph paper with a different *color* for every fifth or tenth line, or breaking the lines up into groups. From here it is just a short step to showing why we have different clefs. Some ingenious student may even

come up with an octave sign.

7) With a full five-line staff, the students can be given enough counters to complete an octave scale. Now is a good time to look at old music with its many different four- or five-line staffs. A discussion may bring out the fact that since most early music was vocal, a five-line staff was sufficient to cover the range of each voice, and it was simpler not to add ledger lines for another voice but to move the clef.

8) From this point on stress may be put on the particular clefs to be used by the student and on taking dictation from the teacher. At first no sharps or flats are used.

Third Stage—Pointers and Observations

This is the stage of acquiring skill and speed, the point where most teachers used to begin the teaching of reading. Much has already been said about it in this discussion.

The third stage begins when the student has gained some familiarity with all of the codes representing musical and technical experiences. It is now time to integrate all of them into a helpful skill which will allow him to become increasingly independent in reading unfamiliar music.

It is also time to begin writing as well as reading. Workbooks are helpful to many, but are not palatable to others. In this stage the teacher should really *flash* the flash cards. It is a time for extended experience with keys, signatures, and compound meters and for ensemble playing, especially if it includes considerable sight reading instead of just mastering a limited performance repertory.

This is the time to give each student confidence to learn to read perfectly. He should be helped to understand the importance of making considerable effort to polish his reading skill Don't take it for granted that students will understand that they *can* learn to read perfectly. Perhaps they have heard of "Uncle Jack, who can play by ear but can't read a note." They may be limited by a similar concept of their own probable future.

It is important that each mark on the page be discussed during the first few weeks of stress on quality reading. If not, the student may mistakenly assume that some of the marks are not important and he will soon stop noticing them. Many violin students, for example, seldom notice the treble clef, and they find with considerable shock, when they begin the viola or the piano, that there are other clefs.

By observation and careful questioning, a parent can come to know which code factors a child may be ignoring purposely. In trying to help him it is wise to start in some area where he is already reasonably successful and help him to develop a very high level of skill in this factor. This will give him self-confidence to go on to tackle weak areas in his reading skill. Octaves may look difficult, but if the student recognizes that they *are* octaves he will only have to read one note.

When accidentals are frequent, the student should become aware of the various possibilities:

1) It may be a minor key.
2) It may be a modulation to another key.
3) The notes may be auxiliaries to the melody, without a real key change.
4) The harmonies may be altered for additional color.
5) The music may lack a key in the traditional sense and be written in one of the twentieth century systems in which a sharp or flat must be indicated every time it appears even within the same measure.

Perceptual Problems may hamper speed reading.

1) The *size* of the notes and the *spacing* on the staff are about equally important in rapid reading. However, spacing does not always relate directly to the relative durations. It is certainly much easier to read when it does!

2) Spacing is hazardous, since all measures in a given meter are equal in length (if the tempo is steady) and yet they may vary from three-eighths of an inch to one and a quarter inches in printed notation. The students' attention should be called to this fact. He must constantly adjust his eye speed.

3) Density of the notes does not always relate to the tempo

of the music. In music written from 1700 to 1825, if the tempo was slow the notes of smaller value were used. An eighth note may have been a very slow note value in an adagio by Handel or Bach. With a quick glance at the printed music the student might be tempted to think it was a fast tempo because it was "so black."

4) There can be confusion in how long a note is held because we say the count at the *beginning* of the beat and not at the end when the note has already been held for one beat. In nearly every other aspect of life we count at the end—years, miles, gallons, inches, etc. The student must retain in his mind the length of time to hold a note even though his eye has moved on.

Ensemble Reading. In playing with a group it is disastrous to give in to the natural tendency to slow down when the music becomes more complicated. Learn to "fake" a bit. Drop some of the notes if necessary. Keep the eye moving steadily and perhaps play only the beginning of each measure for a while, gradually adding the rest of the beats. In preparation, it is very valuable to play with a metronome, consciously playing only the beginning of each measure and keeping a steady rhythm. Then repeat, adding later beats.

Reaction time may be compared to driving. In night driving one uses distance lights to look farther ahead. The student must look farther ahead when playing rapidly, since many more reactions must be started within a short period of time. A very useful device to encourage this is for the teacher or parent to cover the music with a small card in such a way that the student can see a little way ahead of what he is playing but the notes he actually plays are already covered up. This forces him to think two things at the same time, what he is playing (from memory) and what he is about to play (from reading). This is very difficult, but invaluable training to the eye and memory.

Copying Music. One student who learned to read very well had been copying at home some of his music. His mother had suggested that he make a notebook of his favorite pieces, copying them by hand from the printed books. In the process, of course, he learned many very important things. Another student made a thematic catalogue of all the pieces from the first three books, copying just the opening measures of each.

Sharps and Flats, Enharmonic Notes. Interesting musical puzzles can be made up using the enharmonic names for black keys. What is this tune?

$F^b \, C^x \, B^\sharp \, C^x \, F^b \, E \, D^x$ (Mary Had a Little Lamb)

Key Signatures. A mnemonic device for remembering the order of sharps or flats in a key signature is this: (sharps) Father Charles Goes Down And Ends Battle; (flats) Battle Ends And Down Goes Charles' Father.

Transposition. The teacher may dictate letter names of a familiar piece but in a different key from the book. The students try to identify the piece. If done without rhythm this is very difficult.

Rhythmic control is the condition which must always be met in skilled reading. *Tempo, time relationships, technical matters, pressures* from conductor or other players—all of these factors contribute to the difficulties of reading at the highest levels. All reading must be fitted into a pattern where these matters are controlled, and within the student's capacity. Do not expect students to read well material as difficult as their technical level. The reading should be a grade or two easier than the present level of study.

SAMPLES OF ADVICE FROM DR. SUZUKI'S BOOK OF READING EXERCISES *

Goals:

- To understand the fingering when looking at notes without any finger numbers written in—in any position.
- To train the fingers to move at the moment one sees the note. If the fingers move before the brain directs, performance will be poor.
- To sing the fingering smoothly in tempo, looking at the music, in "Lightly Row" or some other similar piece. Until this ability is reached there must be more practice. Ability comes with repetition.
- To count with exactness—at a steady beat.
- To understand thoroughly G Major and G Minor, at first, as the basic violin keys in the first five books. "If you get high ability in one thing, you can get it in others." To play in tune in the fundamental keys is basic. The full range of other keys may come later.
- To see melodic lines as though they were the lines of a design.
- To be able to do the position exercises (four notes each) three times in ten seconds.

"Are you practicing first to learn to play the pieces well and then learning to play them, while counting correctly and musically?"

Methods:

- Say, sing or write notes to a regular beat—usually one written note to two beats of one's pulse, or one sung note or spoken note to each pulse.
- Repeat most drill measures three times, but the harder ones later in the book five times.
- If written work is difficult, write in the answers lightly and erase each day so that it can be done over on succeeding days.

ɔm EXERCISES ON READING NOTES; copyright © 1955 by Zen-On Music Publishers ., Ltd., Tokyo, Japan. All rights reserved. Summy-Birchard Company, Evanston, Illinois, le Selling Agent. Used by permission.

- Every day practice slowly the correct pitch of the 1st and 3rd fingers as basic, then carefully adjust the second finger. Do not neglect intonation while working on reading.
- Take excerpts from the repertory, assigning one particular factor to look for. "There are seven low first and fourth fingers in this excerpt. Can you find them?"
- Practice finding answers quickly. The best way to practice is repetition. We must remember that when we cannot do something, it is because we have not *started* to acquire the ability of doing it. Take the time and the right method and repeat studiously until you get the ability.
- Parents should try to cultivate this spirit of perseverance in children. Don't form the spirit of giving up. If the parents give up, the children will learn to do it, too.
- Throughout all the materials (in the Reading Book) after working out the fingering, switch to counting the music.

At the end of the book, Dr. Suzuki says, "If there is any example you cannot do or find hard to do, go back to the corresponding problem in this book and practice it some more. Those who do this book well will have acquired the ability to read."

† † †

THE TEACHER'S JOB

- To develop and use a specific vocabulary drawn from the symbols printed in the first two or three books while the student learns those pieces by rote. This will lead to awareness of his own experiences, matching vocabulary and later symbols.

*From EXERCISES ON READING NOTES; copyright © 1955 by Zen-On Music Publisher Co., Ltd., Tokyo, Japan. All rights reserved. Summy-Birchard Company, Evanston, Illinoi Sole Selling Agent. Used by permission.

- To draw the mother into the whole reading process, providing advice on how to learn to read the music in the manuals if she does not already know how.
- To make well-reasoned decisions as to when, what, and how to present the various reading concepts and drills.
- To make or purchase such reading aids as are appropriate, and to maintain at least a small lending library of good quality, well-printed music for sight-reading practice by the students.
- To analyze each student's perceptual and physical response factors carefully, give sufficient training to make up for deficiencies, and on occasions make recommendations for professional medical help.
- To excite the student over developing the Three Big Reading Skills listed in a "Reading Creed for Music Students."
- To set conditions or establish rules about reading procedures which will minimize the natural loss of technical control and musical playing which occurs when the student becomes completely involved in reading.

THE PARENT'S JOB

- To work closely with the teacher in developing a compatible approach to reading as used in home practice. This is important for musician-parents.
- To help the student maintain his musical and technical standards when he is too busy reading to notice them. It is most effective to comment frequently on tone, intonation, and hand position—*especially when good!*
- To be on the lookout for distorted postures and seating positions which might indicate perceptual problems or harmful tension.
- To help the child with workbooks, flash cards, and other forms of drill, as well as on reading within a rhythmic framework.

A READING CREED FOR MUSIC STUDENTS

I'll be glad when I don't need help from others to learn new pieces, but can help myself by reading printed music to find exactly what to play and how. When I get stuck, or am careless about how I play while reading, I'll try to be grateful for help from my parents.

I will always do my tonalizing first, before working on reading, in order to get my best listening and playing habits going. I'll end my practice with a fairly easy piece that I can play well and like very much, and play it with my best tone and expressive style.

I will spend at least half of my practice time not looking at music. I will continue to listen to a great deal of the best recorded music. I will never end my practice periods with reading.

I will remember how to sit or stand so that I can see the music without spoiling my posture or playing habits.

I will use Dr. Suzuki's advice that *understanding how to read isn't enough:* that I must take the time, use the right study methods, and repeat any drills until I am an excellent reader.

I will aim for the three big reading skills:

1) *Hearing in my mind the music I study silently before playing.*

2) *Making the music I read send correct messages to my arms and fingers.*

3) *Being able to make musical sound and sense out of printed music I've never heard played.*

† † †

Procedures in Learning an Unfamiliar Solo Without the Help of Records, Book Four Level Students or Higher.

First Principle: When the solo is to be worked up for performance, and is not just for sight-reading practice, it is important to pay attention to every printed detail early in the game since accuracy is essential. To accomplish this, confine each day's practice to a small section of the piece—from one phrase to a page or more, according to the individual's capacities, experience, and the complexity of the material. Take into account the amount which can also be memorized while working on that section. Separate the reading codes and pay attention to one or two at a time, re-combining them until all have been covered.

Second Principle: Remember that codes which are ignored until "later" will cause trouble. A *forte,* or *piano,* for example, should be built into the basic learning of the notes, for notes without expressive content are meaningless.

Third Principle: Don't always start at the beginning but scan through the entire composition, analyzing the tasks ahead. Decide on spots which are most difficult to read so that there will be no reading obstacles to slow down the pace when putting the piece together a little later. Or select passages of obvious technical difficulty which need a head start over the rest of the piece, at the same time devoting time to study mentally the thematic structure of the music.

Fourth Principle: Each day review what was *read* the day before, making sure no code symbols were overlooked. Then work on memorizing that passage. After that, go to work on another section of the piece, but do try the newly memorized sections over again once or twice more during the practice. After two or three days, it should be possible to gauge how much work can be accomplished in the week, and to chart out the remaining work. Deadlines, if not rigid, give a sense of purpose to anyone's work. Begin to put the parts together after a few days, much like a jig-saw puzzle, in order to get the sound picture. Clear up spots which are not understood or mark with a question to ask at the next lesson. Remember that even if every single mark is correctly understood, only correct actions can bring the pieces to musical life. Start making a habit of the actions which produce the desired results.

A Sample Day's Practice on a Section of a New Piece

1) Select the section after having first looked through the whole piece, locating tempo marks and changes, and any terms which indicate the general character of the music. Locate the principle divisions of the piece, noting repetitions or variations of the themes. Mark them, preferably with alphabet letters for each theme. Use a music dictionary, or even a standard unabridged English one to find the meaning of terms not understood.

2) Work out the rhythm and the accent pattern which goes with the meter. Choose a sensible beat and keep it steady while tapping or tonguing (ta, ta, etc.) the rhythm. Count it, too, in whatever way you know.

3) Study the notes, first looking at the sharps or flats in the key signature. If you know that key, play the scale and notice where the half-steps are. String students should mark the half-steps in the first two or three lines to insure correct spacings so that the sound of the key becomes quickly established. (Mistakes may then be recognized more easily in the parts which follow.) Try singing the themes.

4) Say each note's name aloud. Also say the fingering aloud, and add the position name if learning the higher positions. Dr. Suzuki suggests doing this kind of thing at a speed of one note per beat at the tempo of one's own pulse. Repeat several times. Remember to do this at an even tempo, disregarding the regular rhythm.

5) Transfer the fingering to a dummy keyboard or table if a pianist, or to a stringed instrument with the left hand only,

practicing silently.

6) Combine the fingering with the correct rhythm, now, trying to maintain a steady tempo—probably a slow one. String students should pantomime the bowing without holding a bow. Add dynamics to the pantomime, varying the forcefulness and speed of the arm motion.

7) Next, play the music on the instrument, putting the day's section together so far as categories of symbols to be followed. Mark the spots that obviously need extra practice.

8) Practice these spots and then play straight through again, trying to use the dynamics, the textures, the tempo changes, as well as bringing out phrase groupings.

9) Pantomime the whole section once more, with good rhythm and expressive gestures to match the character and style of the piece.

10) Play straight through once more, trying to combine as many of the skills as possible. Test to see how much has been memorized in the process of reading and working on the motions.

The unique type of group recital developed by Dr. Suzuki brings together students at all stages of achievement for the pleasure of sharing their repertory. The more difficult numbers are programmed first.

Appendix

Elizabeth Mills

A Self-Examination for Talent Education Parents

What are my sources of strength in relation to my child's music?

Why am I having him study music?

What is *my* value hierarchy for his school work, his "character building" activities, his hobbies, his social activities, his free time, and his music?

What is *his* value hierarchy and how do we reconcile any differences?

Do I profess one goal and choose behavior more suitable for another?

If there are conflicting attitudes among members of the household on this matter of music study, how do I handle it?

Am I happy with my child? Do I resent his ways: his slowness, his energy, his stubbornness, his talkativeness, his curiosity, or even his brightness?

Do I help him channel and develop the qualities which make him unique, rather than try to turn him into something he is not?

How do I nourish my child and myself musically?

Do I buy the recommended records? Have I included these as real necessities in the study budget? Do I work them in as a regular part of the study, and often listen with my child with an attitude of interest and pleasure?

Do I attend concerts and take my child to appropriate musical events? Do I take advantage of the many fine free or low cost concerts by advanced students in the area colleges?

Do I spend time and effort, as well as money, making sure the tonal reproduction my child hears is the best we can manage? That the needle and record surfaces are protected and cared for?

Do I buy or borrow from a library additional records for pleasure?

Am I making regular, unpressured practice possible?

Have I solved the problem of a good place to practice, allowing for some walking about?

Do I see that the practice time is planned, and if possible in two or more segments rather than one long period? Do I also remain flexible enough to find alternatives?

Do I help the development of practice plans for these times?

Do I provide an appreciative listening ear during practice?

Do I help my child remember the motions and techniques the teacher worked on? Do I learn how to help my child move with my physical assistance, as the teacher often does?

Do I make helpful specific comments which include solutions?

Not this: "That's terribly out of tune!"

But this: "Do you think it is out of tune because your hand is tight, or because you're not sure of the finger pattern?

In what ways am I encouraging my child?

Do I take my child to the extra classes and recitals planned by his teacher for additional training, experience, or stimulation?

Do we discuss the positive side of other students' work and growth after leaving such events? (A critical attitude of other students implies potential threatening criticism of my own child).

Do I keep "extrinsic" rewards to a minimum?

Do I make music part of recreation in our home in at least one way?

Do I record his progress from time to time, perhaps with a movie camera showing his motions, a still camera showing basic playing postures or tape recordings for his sound at regular intervals on one special tape kept for that purpose?

Do I buy him the best "tools" I can afford, and see that he has good quality strings that are changed as they become false or frayed, good rosin in usable shape, clean bow hair that is rehaired as it becomes worn, and any other accessories recommended by the teacher?

Do I make music (not practice) a part of normal conversation in our home?

Have I made a habit of finding things to like about the music he plays (even if simple)? (Any performer is happy when someone comments on liking a particular composition). Do I avoid the "not that again" look, and educate the rest of the family to do the same? Do I read some musical reviews in the newspapers and share any interesting comments? (I can at least learn musical jargon and attitudes this way, even if I did not hear the concerts being reviewed).

Do I keep in mind that my tone of voice when talking to my child about his music or that of others may make him uncomfortable or comfortable about music in general, discouraged or encouraged about his own?

How am I growing?

Am I becoming more musical myself?

Do I find myself enjoying various aspects of it increasingly?

Do I understand violin problems better than before?

Am I gaining in understanding children and their needs?

Is my child aware of my growth, or do I unwittingly give the impression that adults are saints who have completed their growth to a level that he must also reach someday (and never go beyond)? Do I find subtle ways to draw attention to my improvements so that he can more easily cope with his own mistakes without discouragement?

Have I tried to achieve desirable goals, but had a sense of failure?

Have I sought help from other more experienced mothers (in point of supervising music study), or from my child's teacher?

* * * * * *

If the number of "yes" answers doesn't seem high enough, try finding solutions by re-reading the questions, substituting some of the following for "Do I," etc.: Should I? Will I? Why don't I?

Questions and Answers

At seven different meetings with seven sets of parents, I showed the video-tapes (which we recorded in Japan in October 1971, with the equipment you are helping us purchase). These were but a small portion of the many tapes we made of violin and piano lessons and nursery school sessions at the Talent Education Institute in Matsumoto. Dr. Suzuki was shown demonstrating what he feels are vital points about bowing. Younger teachers were shown with their students. Mothers could be seen entering into the lessons, often with parallel motions to the teacher's.

The parent discussions which were provoked were quite similar. The summary which follows includes the major questions asked and some of my comments.

* * * * * *

If parent-child learning teams have not been developed to a high degree by age 8, is it too late? What about our older beginners and our students who have been working independently for a long time with the only parental involvement being financial and a matter of transportation?

I think we should improve in this area! Good patterns are worth striving for any time, even though easier to build from scratch. Since we are not talking about scratch, let's take heart from the fact that one has to build new patterns anyway as a child grows older. He is bound to OUTGROW whatever has worked well at an early age. *We should worry if signs of independence* do not appear around age 8. This is true the world over, and no one recognizes it more than Dr. Suzuki.

One day, when a group of half a dozen Americans in Matsumoto were wishing American children were as teachable as the children we were observing, Dr. Suzuki said nothing for awhile. Then he said warmly, "I like American children. They have such high spirits." I think we do excel in developing spontaneity, and this is important too.

It is a great advantage for the older student if he can accept help in at least a few areas—no one can see or hear himself as others do (although our video camera is beginning to help). Parents need to make every effort to become involved with what their children are doing and achieving in their teen years. This must be done in ways that will not be crippling, of course, either through creating too much pressure or too much dependency. Don't back away permanently when an older child verbally seems to reject your unsolicited advice. But do find ways to encourage him to SOLICIT your advice in areas which currently concern him.

In skill areas like dance, sports and music, one way to avoid the possibility that your child won't reach his potential is to pay for more time from the teacher or other professional help. Since few can afford this, parents should realize their own potential for teaching. Not only will they help their child by pointing out specifics, but they will come to enjoy the skill-art themselves even more. The great disadvantage of paying someone else to be the sole mentor is the loss of that special joy which results when a mother or father share in depth the little and the big steps which a child takes, and which can only be appreciated by people who have watched progress closely with an encouraging rather than a pressuring attitude.

What seemed to be the relation between adult expectations and children's achievements?

I saw great evidence that Dr. Suzuki's goals had also become the goals of an amazing percentage of teachers and parents. He has worked long and persistently to establish an ideal which emphasized educating both musically and academically in a manner that will bring out the noblest spirit in man. High heart is given more importance than high fame.

In educating all who sincerely seek help, Dr. Suzuki still sets very high standards and demands a great deal. He tolerates as temporary each student's shortcomings, but goes right on helping him reach those high standards with patience and good humor. The very fact that he assumes they will reach a high level certainly seems to have a bearing on the children's achievements, and on the parents' belief in their children's potentials.

In the absence of a competitive spirit, what motivations were apparent?

While pride in achievement for the sake of a family name may still serve as a powerful motivator for many in Japan (and in the best circumstances helps a child work for a goal outside of himself). I saw an excitement and eagerness among the children which seemed to come from two things: first, from just simple enjoyment of what they were doing, from music itself; second, from the propelling force which doing a thing well seems to generate.

Perhaps, most important of all, the child's need to have models to imitate is well-known. This idea is everywhere evident. Little pianists, listening to bigger pianists in recitals or lessons, were busy "fingering" along. Little violinists pantomimed along with others. And little nursery schoolers imitated the beautiful manners of older nursery schoolers, for they do not separate 3, 4, and 5 year olds in the Institute nursery school. Dr. Suzuki said to me, "Already the three year olds have had six months education in good manners from four and five year olds who have had six months to learn how to be kind to three year olds." This is his plan. Very simple—if adults agree on a good curriculum and a good method.

What price this achievement? What about freedom and spontaneity and creativity?

These goals are more important in our culture than in the traditional Japanese. However, they are experimenting with our ideas and we should certainly feel free to reciprocate. I don't think we need to kill a child's natural inventiveness or creativity while helping him develop technical skills for high quality work. What is wrong with giving a creative child the tools which can only be achieved through the orderly, persistent efforts we refer to as discipline? I kept seeing evidence there, and see it here, which points to the wisdom of developing a child's tools as early as possible. It doesn't matter what he will do with them later. Giving him a violin, for example, does not mean that all is wasted when the instrument does not seem to appeal to him a few years later. Most children have great "transfer" ability.

If a child does not naturally use his abilities in a creative way by the time he is seven or eight, perhaps we can find ways to aid him in getting on that track which is so natural around that age. An example from Japan comes to my mind of children making creative use of tools acquired. The "graduates" of Dr. Suzuki's nursery school have been entering public school at 6 with an average I.Q. of as high as 169 some years. He feels this is in part due to the great amount of emphasis on memory training—which we often feel makes it difficult to be creative or to think for oneself. Each child is expected to memorize 200 Haiku verses. A public school teacher reported that many of these children fill the margins of their quickly finished math papers with their own Haiku poems.

Where do we go from here?

Are we all growing? Parents? Teachers? Older students? Younger students? Are we enjoying the process most of the time? Are we helping each other enjoy it? Are we learning more about life through trying to conquer a complex skill? And at the same time, are we letting the art of music get through to ourselves? That is the point at which we will find the sustenance for the journey down a very long road.

209

Recitals in Suzuki Style

(Explanation for Visitors to Programs)

The unique type of group recital developed by Dr. Suzuki brings together people at all stages of achievement for the pleasure of playing some of their shared repertory together. Since this is solo literature, precise ensemble and identical interpretations are not the primary goals and only the opening and closing of each piece are conducted by a teacher. Starting with the more difficult numbers, the programs proceed to progressively easier pieces played by increasing numbers of students, with everyone joining in the finale—the rhythm variations by Dr. Suzuki on Twinkle, Twinkle Little Star. Thus, the beginners joining in feel the assurance that comes from having watched more experienced students first.

Why should solos be played in unison? This question can best be answered by asking other questions. In what other way could so many students gain security in such matters as memory, tempo, adaptability, and technical and psychological stamina in a fairly extensive repertory? Experience has shown that most students do not become dependent upon this group playing, but gain confidence and the desire to perform alone. And how else could the repeated review of earlier repertory, so necessary for control and polish, be made pleasant for so many students, at the same time helping them maintain and build an available supply of solo material.

Some of the other benefits may be listed, too. One intrinsic reward is the awareness of one's own improvement. Another is an understanding of the importance of continual work for improvement over a long period of time. The integration of new skills into the repertory previously learned is still another, and one which requires alertness, thus helping prevent merely mechanical playing. Motivation for the younger students is provided as they hear the literature ahead, and older students become interested in the growth process as they observe the younger students negotiating the early hurdles. The general atmosphere is of a community of students, families, and teachers devoted to creating musical beauty with ever increasing skill.

Bibliography

SUZUKI TEACHING METHODS AND MATERIALS

Violin

Suzuki Violin School. Volumes 1 through 6 (Rev. Bilingual Ed.) Violin and Piano accompaniment in separate books. 12" LP record albums for Vols. 1–2, 3–4, 5, & 6.

Volumes 7 through 10–(Original Ed.). Violin and Piano accompaniment in separate books.

Duets for Two Violins: Second Violin Parts to Selections from Suzuki Violin School (Rev. Ed.). Vols. 1, 2, & 3.

Home Concert
Pieces arranged by Shinichi Suzuki for either violin solo or ensemble. Violin parts and piano accompaniment.

Listen and Play by John Kendall
Books 1, 2, & 3, with accompaniment books and 12" LP record album for Books 1–2, & 3. Contents of the three books parallel Suzuki Vols. 1 & 2, but include supplementary materials, practice suggestions for teachers, and illustrations.

Suzuki in the String Class by Paul Zahtilla.
Teachers Manual, Violin, Viola, Cello, and Bass Books. 12" LP record album for each instrument book. Contents parallel Vol. 1 of Suzuki Violin School through "Etude."

All the above materials are distributed by Summy-Birchard Company—Evanston, Ill. 60204. Sole publisher and agent for North America by special arrangement with Zen-On Music Company Ltd.

Violoncello

Sato, Yoshio. Sato Cello School: The Suzuki Method. Evanston, Ill.: Summy-Birchard Co., 1969. 2 Volumes. (Volumes 3-4 in preparation.)

Piano

Suzuki Piano School, Evanston, Ill.: Summy-Birchard Co., 4 Volumes with 2 LP Recordings. (Volumes 5, 6, & 7 in preparation.)

BIBLIOGRAPHY

MISCELLANEOUS MATERIALS

Cook, Clifford. "Suzuki Education in Action." Jericho, N.Y. Exposition Press.

Kendall, John, "Talent Education and Suzuki." (Pamphlet) Washington, D.C. Music Educators National Conference publication.

Suzuki, Shinichi. "Nurtured by Love." Jericho, N. Y. Exposition Press. *(Required Reading.)*

"Progress Report" forms. Available from Mihoko Yamaguchi Hirata, 621 Harvard Ave. E., Seattle, Wash. 98102.

"Vital Points." Illustrated pamphlet with pictures showing good and bad bowing positions—for home use. Available also from Mrs. Hirata. *(Required reading for new parents and teachers.)*

SUPPLEMENTARY MUSICAL MATERIALS FOR STRINGS

For Learning to Read Fingering:
"Johnson Violin Method." Kjos Music Co., Park Ridge, Illinois.
"Fun with a Fiddle." George Perlman, Carl Fischer, New York.

For Learning to Think Letter Names on the Fingerboard:
"Rainbow Tunes." Modern Music Methods. Ogden, Utah. In multi-color "now" design, this book is enjoyed by students as a change, and as a step to reading by students started by rote. Good for the teacher's loan library. Letters rather than numbers used.

For Reading Practice:
"String Reader." Bornoff, George. Carl Fischer, New York. The three sections use a rhythm variation approach, with considerable challenge to observe bowing and rhythm factors. First section is in large notes. All strings.

"Doflein Method." Erich and Elma. G. Schirmer Inc. New York. Five books of the best quality music, carefully graded. 16th century to Bartok and Hindemith. Short technical studies, solos and duets. (For violin.)

"Solo Time for Strings." Forrest Etling. Pub. by Etling, 1790 Joseph Court, Elgin, Illinois. 60120. All strings.

"Above the First Position." Markwood Holmes and Russel Webber. C. Fischer, New York.

"Albumstücke." Dmitri Kabalevsky. Peters (German edition). Most of the pieces were written for piano but have been adapted by the composer for violin. Good pedagogical points and several excellent pieces for performance as well as for sight-reading experience.

"Folk Tunes in Fiddle Finger Forms." Howard Koch. Boston Music Co., Boston. First book is devoted to the "close 2-3 position" of the fingers. The second book completes the key and position cycle.

BIBLIOGRAPHY

"Rhythm and Bowings." Pub. Neil Kjos, Park Ridge, Illinois.

"New Tunes for Strings." Paul Rosen and Margaret Rowell. Music, Inc., Suite 611, 1841 Broadway, New York, 10023.

Ensembles:

"Fiddle Sessions—Fun for Two, Three and Four Violins." Elizabeth Green and Livingston Gearharts. Shawnee Press. Delaware Water Gap, Penna.

Music-Minus-One record and music book sets:

Besides the extensive catalog of concerto accompaniments and chamber music with one part missing, several records are available for the less advanced students. These include both parts, with the stereo separation permitting one speaker to be turned down or off so that the opposite part may be heard separately and then reversing the process to hear the other part.

Applebaum. "Beautiful Music for Two Violins" (also Viola and Cello versions). 4 Volumes. Bartok. "44 Violin Duos." 2 Volumes. Pleyel. "Duos, op. 8, numbers 1, 2 and 6."

Technique:

"Contemporary Technique." Galamian and Neumann. Galaxy, New York. Scales and arpeggios presented by fingering categories, and with a variation approach combining bowing and rhythm variations. Suzuki students will find it a very natural approach. The inclusion of non-traditional contemporary scale forms increases the usefulness.

"Dictionary of Bowing Terms." Berman and Seagrave. American String Teachers' Association. Order from Paul Rolland, Univ. of Illinois, Urbana, Ill. This book is not only informative, it is good reading.

"Violin Left Hand Technique." Neumann. American String Teachers' Assn. This is a very thorough discussion of every aspect of left hand work. After considerable material is given on the options possible in each aspect and on the famous violinists who have subscribed to each of the options, Mr. Neumann presents his own common sense conclusions.

Workbooks:

"Workbook for Strings." Forrest Etling. Published by Etling, listed above. Two volumes for each of the stringed instruments.

"Sound and Symbol." Green and Pooler. Pro-art, New York. A basic theory book with excellent practical assignments for the student playing in junior high or high school orchestras.

"Music Flash Cards." Ted Ross. Charles Hansen Music Corp., Miami Beach, Fla. 5½x8½ cards arranged progressively in four sets of forty each. Should be purchased complete and arranged according to categories. All types of symbols included, and the treble clef notes go down to low E.

"Music Workbook for Strings." Phyllis Rowe. Summy-Birchard, Evanston, Ill. Well presented material for upper elementary age.

BIBLIOGRAPHY

BOOKS USEFUL TO TEACHERS AND PARENTS

Brazelton, T. "Infants and Mothers." New York. Delacorte Press, 1969. Jerome Bruner, in the foreword says, "Babies from the start go about the achievement of growth in such different ways. Dr. Brazelton has very wisely chosen to present the contrast between the very active, the moderately active, and the quiet baby. . . He invites us to be courteous to the infants who are our children. . . And he halps us to achieve courtesy by sketching the range of individual expression that infancy can take."

Beadle, M. "A Child's Mind—How Children Learn During the Critical Years from Birth to Age Five." Garden City, N.Y. Doubleday. 1971.

Bruner, J. "Toward a Theory of Instruction." New York. W. W. Norton & Co. 1968. The insights of this author are among the most valuable in the field of education. All of his writings are highly recommended.

Chall, J. "Learning to Read—The Great Debate." New York. McGraw-Hill, 1967. An inquiry into the science, art, and ideology of old and new methods of teaching children to read from 1910-1965. Essentially a technical book for educators, but useful to anyone interested in the subject.

Doman, G. "How to Teach your Baby to Read—The Gentle Revolution." N.Y. Random House, 1964. If brain-damaged children can benefit tremendously from early reading work, what about normal children? This is the substance of Doman's work, and his final chapter, "On Joyousness," should be MUST reading for Suzuki parents.

Gariepy, R. "Your Child Is Dying to Learn!" Barre, Mass. Barre Pub. 1967. Much material about Suzuki is included by this writer who agrees with and appreciates Suzuki's view of learning. "It comes as startling fact to realize that our educational system and entire process of teaching children is based on several myths. The most unforgivable of these is the theory that certain youngsters are born highly *intelligent* and the vast majority are not!" A psychologist's approach.

Ginott, H. "Between Parent and Child." New York. Hearst Corp. 1965. Giving parents a language approach similar to that of professional medical people and therapists in the interaction between children and adults is a real contribution to home life—and should do much to prevent emotional disorders. Later books carry the approach on to the teen-ager, and the teacher.

Gordon, T. "Parent Effectiveness Training." New York. Peter Wyden Inc. 1970. This book is used as a text in a widespread program of school and community sponsored training classes for parents. Gordon says that, "parents have been blamed but not trained." A book for teacher effectiveness follows.

Hall, E. "The Silent Language." Greenwich, Conn. Fawcett Pub., 1959. The factor of communication outside of the spoken language is given good treatment here. Every adult will benefit from reading this book carefully.

Holt, J. "How Children Learn." New York. Dell Pub. Co., 1967. This sequel to "How Children Fail" is useful for those who would understand the meaning, in learning terms, of young children's behaviour.

Hainstock, E. "Teaching Montessori in the Home—The Pre-School Years." New York. Random House, 1968. Instructions for making equipment and doing learning experiments at home.

Isaacs, N. "A Brief Introduction to Piaget." New York. Agathon Press, 1972. An excellent introduction to the insights of this important psychologist for those not interested in delving into the more complex and professional writings of Piaget.

Markel, R. "Guide to Music Education." New York. Macmillan Co. 1972. Good general advice for music study, mostly of a traditional kind, but including Suzuki psychology. Includes all instruments, what to look for in a good teacher, business policies, etc. One of the best of its type to appear.

Montessori, M. "The Absorbent Mind." New York. Dell Pub., 1967. "In the present volume Dr. Montessori not only sheds the light of her penetrating insight, based on close observation and just evaluation, on the phenomena of this earliest and yet most decisive period of human life, but also indicates the responsibility of adult humanity towards it. She, indeed, gives a practical meaning to the new universally accepted necessity of 'education from birth'."

Nordoff, P., and Robbins, C. "Therapy in Music for Handicapped Children." New York. St. Martin's Press, Inc. 1971. Very useful for teachers wishing to understand types of handicaps and the personality aspects of each, as well as the creative approach these men used in their music therapy work.

Pines, M. "Revolution In Learning—The Years From Birth to Six." New York. Harper and Row. 1966. Persuasive material on early educational development.

Post, E. "Please, Say Please—A Common Sense Guide to Bringing Up Your Child." Dr. Suzuki gives much attention to the subject of respect—of the teacher for the child and of child for teacher. Mrs. Post's book is based on her philosophy, "Good manners are based on thoughtfulness for others, and their primary aim is to make human relationships as smooth and pleasant as possible. Furthermore, the person whose manners are natural and unpretentious is an attractive person, and blessed with self-confidence and self-respect."

BIBLIOGRAPHY

Salk, L. and Kramer, R. "How to Raise a Human Being." New York, Harper. 1969. The authors draw on clinical experience and the latest research to demonstrate the crucial importance of directing the child's early experiences, which could determine how he develops later in life. Covers infancy through adolescence. Besides discussing the needs of each period, they discuss the need for parents to find their own ways of caring for different types of children.

A SAMPLING OF BOOKS FOR SUZUKI VIOLIN STUDENTS

Chapin V. "The Violin and Its Masters." New York. J. B. Lippincott Co. 1969.
Ewen D. "Famous Instrumentalists." New York. Dodd, Mead & Co. 1965.
Gammond, P. "The Meaning and Magic of Music." New York. Golden Press. 1970.
Gough, C. "Boyhoods of Great Composers." New York. Henry A. Walck. 1965.
Layton, R. "Sibelius." New York. Viking Press.
Mirsky, R. "Johann Sebastian Bach." Chicago. Follett Pub. Co. 1965.
Mondadori, A. ed. "The Life and Times of Chopin." Phila. Curtis Pub. Co. 1967.
Nelson, S. "The Violin and Viola." New York. W. W. Norton & Co. 1972.
Neumann, W. "Bach and His World." New York. Viking Press.
Rosell, E. Z. "American Composers." New York. Houghton Mifflin. 1963.
Poulsson, E. "Finger Plays." New York. Dover Pub., Inc. 1971.
Seroff, V. "Wolfgang Amadeus Mozart." New York. Macmillan Co. 1965.
Valentin, E. "Beethoven." New York. Viking Press.
Wechsberg, J. "The Glory of the Violin." New York. Viking Press. 1972.
Wechsberg, J. "The Story of Music." New York. Pantheon Books. 1968.

A 32-page booklet, *In the Suzuki Style,* is available from Diablo Press. It includes words for the songs of Book I, practical projects for string students at the holiday season, first note and key information for playing carols by ear, a section on how to tune the violin, and other vital information for students and parents. To obtain this booklet, send $1 to Diablo Press, 462 Coventry Road, Berkeley, California. (Californians add sales tax.)